Greed Addiction

Why Power Is the Most Dangerous Drug on Earth

Samina Rose

Greed Addiction

ISBN: 979-8-9882468-7-9

Allegra Publishing

Contents

About the Author i
Preface ii
PART I: GREED AS AN ADDICTION 2
Chapter 1: What Is Greed? 3
A Pattern Across History 3
Greed as Symbol 6
Need Is Not Greed 7
The Addiction Pattern 8
The Psychological Layer Beneath 9
When Greed Becomes Social 9
A Different Question 11
References 12
Chapter 2: When Greed Becomes Power 15
Greed and Power Are Not the Same 15
Power as Expansion 16
Power as Protection 17
Power as Normalization 18
From Behavior to System 19
A Structural Loop 19
Toward the Inner Layer 20
References 20
Chapter 3: The Neurology of "Never Enough" 22
Dopamine Is Not Happiness 23
The Brain Learns to Chase Cues and Reaches Tolerance 24
If Dopamine Drives Wanting, What Produces Contentment? 25
The Conflict Between Pursuit and Contentment 27
Social Comparison and Hierarchy 28
Stress and the Biology of Scarcity 29
Trauma and the Rejected Self 30

Rejection and Social Pain....31
Why "More" Never Resolves the Void.... 31
A Society Built on Neural Vulnerabilities.... 32
References....34
PART II: THE PSYCHOLOGY OF GREED-ADDICTION.. 37
Chapter 4: The Fragile Core: Greed as a Coping Mechanism.... 38
The Wound Beneath the Armor, and the Manufactured Mask....39
The Addiction Pattern.... 42
What healing actually is (and what the end goal is).... 44
Narcissism and the Fear of Insignificance.... 45
Common Narcissistic Coping Strategies....46
A Fragile Foundation....49
References....50
Chapter 5: Emotional Numbing and The Mask of Success.... 52
Two Nervous Systems, One Strategy....53
The Mask of Success.... 54
Making Beautiful Ugly and Ugly Beautiful....55
CRC-PTSD and the Performative Self....56
Greed, Gender, and the Policing of Identity....57
The End Goal: Matching Energy, Not Masks....58
References....59
Chapter 6: Trauma Bond And Bystander Effect.... 61
1) Trauma bonding: attachment under threat....61
2) The system-level version: institutions as trauma-bonding machines....63
3) The bystander effect: when conscience is outsourced....63
4) How these two patterns reinforce each other....64
5) What this does to the soul: CRC-PTSD as a social outcome.... 65
6) Breaking the loop: the Truth-Teller intervention....66
7) The political meaning of intervention.... 68
References.... 68
Chapter 7: Addiction Escalation: Power....71

1. The Psychological Angle: Control as a Substitute for Belonging....71
2. The Attachment Angle: Avoiding the Cost of Dependence..72
3. The Neurobiological Angle: Escalation, Tolerance, and the Plateau....73
4. The Moral Angle: Empathy Becomes a Threat.... 74
5. The Economic Angle: When Growth Becomes a Withdrawal Avoidance....75
6. The Cultural Angle: The Empire of Comparison.... 76
7. Long-Term Effects: What Happens If This Continues?.... 77
8. The Intervention: Rebuilding Connection as a Form of Recovery....79
References.... 80
PART III: How We Celebrate An Illness....81
Chapter 8: Greed Produced Scarcity.... 82
The Historical Roots of Manufactured Scarcity....83
Law as Pseudo-Science, Patents as Knowledge Control, and the Gaslighting of Inner Knowing.... 85
Scarcity as an Ideology.... 87
The Language of Scarcity.... 88
Scarcity and the Commodification of the Self....89
The Political Function of Scarcity.... 90
References.... 91
Chapter 9: The Myth of Personal Responsibility....93
Life Is Not a Single Moment — It's a compounding Timeline.94
Human-Made Merit Units....95
An Addict: "Bad Choices" or a Rigged Nervous System?....97
A Homeless Person: The "Bad Decision" Myth.... 98
The Full-Time Worker: Working and Still Falling Behind....99
The Double-Job Worker: Discipline Becomes a Trap.... 99
Poor and Rich: The Same Action, Different Moral Meaning.100
The Deep Function of the Myth.... 101
The Truth That Breaks the Spell.... 101
What This Chapter Is Asking You to See....102
References....103

Chapter 10: Greed as a Systemic Addiction..................104
1. When "More" Becomes Non-Negotiable............................ 104
2. Corruption as a Design Feature, Not an Exception............105
3. How the System Trains the Human Nervous System........106
4. The Feedback Loop That Makes Greed Systemic...............107
5. The Long-Term Future of a Greed-Addicted System.........108
6. The Solution: How Humans Free Themselves...................109
7. The Truth-Teller as the First Antidote............................... 112
References...113
Chapter 11: The Trauma of the 90%..............................114
PART IV: BREAKING THE ADDICTION....................... 121
Chapter 12: How Can We Recover?.............................122
1) Truth-Teller Recovery Starts with the Nervous System.....123
2) Fasting from the System's Inputs......................................124
3) Dancing Instead of Speaking: Returning to the Body's Language... 125
4) Silence as a Technology of Truth......................................127
5) "Unbelieving Money" Without Falling into Harm............128
6) Don't Cram Life Into One Box...130
7) Learn Life from Animals Again..131
8) Play Like a Child... 132
9) Imagination as Prayer—and Why "The Law of Attraction" Must Become Collective..132
10) What Recovery Looks Like at Scale.................................133
11) The End Goal... 134
Chapter 13: Replacing "More" With "Enough"............136
1) The material foundation of "enough"................................ 136
2) Independent living: not the fantasy, the design.................137
3) Staying connected online while living close to land.......... 140
4) Finding people you "Vibe with" and then physically connecting...141
Safety Without the Mask...142
References.. 143

About the Author

Samina Rose is a writer and theorist whose work examines how modern systems manufacture scarcity, normalize institutional betrayal, and convert human worth into economic measurement. Drawing from lived experience, trauma-informed frameworks, and sociological critique, she develops language for the psychological injuries created by bureaucracy, capitalism, and relational injustice—especially when people are forced to mask their humanity in order to survive.

She is the author of *The Truth Teller: Reforming Our World*, *Compounded Relational cPTSD: The Truth-Teller's Path*, and *What Happened to Humanity?* Her writing introduces concepts such as the Truth-Teller Paradigm and Compounded Relational c-PTSD (CRC-PTSD) to describe how repeated interpersonal and institutional harms accumulate over time and reshape identity, safety, and meaning. Her work centers a simple conviction: truth-telling is not only personal—it is political, relational, and necessary for collective healing.

Samina was trained as a midwife in Iran and later immigrated to the United States, where she encountered the bureaucratic and credential systems that often erase lived competence and replace it with gatekeeping. She writes at the intersection of psychology, sociology, and moral philosophy, with a focus on restoring human dignity beyond productivity, wealth, and social status.

Preface

We live in a society where money has become more important than human lives. When a society builds its definitions of worth around wealth, productivity, and status, the result is not only inequality; it is a population trained into chronic insecurity, comparison, masking, and emotional numbing. The vice becomes the engine. The symptom becomes the standard. And human lives become collateral damage. Greed is framed as success. Changing that frame is an urgent matter.

The core claim of this book is simple and unsettling: **greed behaves like an addiction**, and **power is the instrument that allows that addiction to scale into social architecture**. Greed seeks more; power secures the conditions through which "more" can be pursued without limit. Once greed attaches to power, it stops being merely personal. It becomes structural: housing becomes investment, healthcare becomes a market, work becomes extraction, and "never enough" becomes the psychological climate most people breathe without even realizing it.

I am not writing this as a detached observer. I am writing as someone who has lived inside systems that repeatedly demand self-erasure in exchange for survival, and who has watched how institutional logic can train people to doubt their own reality, mistrust their own needs, and blame themselves for conditions they did not create. In my earlier work, I named the cumulative psychic injury of these conditions as **Compounded Relational c-PTSD (CRC-PTSD)**—not as a private diagnosis, but as a social outcome of chronic relational harm across institutions. This book is one more attempt to put the blame where it belongs: not on individuals for "failing," but on the structures that manufacture insecurity and then sell self-optimization as salvation.

The chapters move through three layers. First, we define greed across moral traditions, mythology, and language, because human beings have warned about this force for centuries—even when modern systems pretend it is virtuous. Then we examine the neurology of "never enough," not to reduce greed to brain chemistry, but to give scientific ground for those criticizing this old wisdom. From there, we enter the psychological and relational core: how shame, masking, and the fear of insignificance can make accumulation feel like safety—until power replaces connection and the addiction escalates.

I don't want this book to end in despair or in clinical diagnosis. The later sections turn toward recovery—toward what it would mean for a system to heal, and for human beings to unhook themselves from the trance of "never enough." That recovery begins where modern culture rarely looks: in the body. It begins by calming down enough to hear what we already know, and by fasting from the inputs that keep the addiction running—comparison, panic cycles, and the daily narrative that you are behind. From there, it moves into practices that restore our humanity: ceremony, presence, play, shared care, and forms of belonging where people can be real without punishment.

If you take one thing from this book, let it be this: the opposite of greed is not sacrifice. It is **enough**—materially, relationally, and spiritually. And the opposite of domination is not powerlessness. It is shared human flourishing. A greed-addicted system survives by making people feel unsafe without masks. Recovery begins the moment we build lives—together—where it is possible to feel safe without masks. Where we can be as honest, caring and sharing as children we are all inside.

GREED ADDICTION

Samina Rose

PART I

GREED AS AN ADDICTION

CHAPTER 1

What Is Greed?

Greed is something deeper than selfishness.

It is a compulsion to accumulate beyond need—sustained by psychological reward and reinforced by social systems that treat accumulation as success.

In this sense, greed behaves less like a moral flaw and more like an addiction.

A Pattern Across History

Across cultures, time periods, and belief systems, greed has been recognized with striking consistency—not merely as desire, but as a destabilizing force when left without limits.

In ancient Greek philosophy, greed was captured by the concept of *pleonexia*, often translated as "the desire to have more." But its meaning extended beyond simple accumulation. Pleonexia referred specifically to taking more than one's fair share, often at the expense of others and the collective good (Balot 2001). Plato and Aristotle both identified this impulse as a central cause of injustice and political instability. When individuals pursue private gain without regard for social balance, the foundations of communal life begin to erode (Plato 1992; Aristotle 1999). In this framework, greed is not merely personal excess—it is a threat to the stability of the entire political order.

A similar concern appears across the Abrahamic traditions. In Judaism, greed is often expressed through the concept of covetousness—the desire to possess what belongs to others. The Hebrew Bible repeatedly warns against the pursuit of wealth at the expense of justice, emphasizing fairness in trade, protection of the vulnerable, and moral responsibility toward the community (Brueggemann 2014). In this tradition, the problem is not wealth itself, but the distortion of ethical relationships that occurs when accumulation overrides justice.

In Christianity, greed is traditionally referred to as avarice, one of the Seven Deadly Sins. Avarice is not simply the desire for wealth, but an immoderate love of riches that displaces moral concern for others (Aquinas 1947; Newhauser 2000). The figure of the "rich fool" in the Gospel of Luke illustrates this clearly: a man who stores up wealth for himself without regard for others is ultimately portrayed as spiritually impoverished. Here, greed becomes a form of misalignment—placing material gain above human and spiritual obligations.

Islamic thought similarly distinguishes between lawful wealth and excessive attachment to it. The concept of *ḥirṣ* refers to an intense craving or eagerness for wealth and status that exceeds moderation. Islamic teachings emphasize balance through practices such as zakat, a structured redistribution of wealth intended to prevent extreme inequality and ensure social responsibility (Kuran 2004). In this framework, greed is not the possession of wealth, but the failure to circulate it in ways that sustain collective wellbeing.

Across these traditions, a consistent pattern emerges:
Wealth is not condemned, but hoarding is.

What is rejected is the accumulation of resources in ways that harm others or sever responsibility to the community.

In Eastern traditions, greed is conceptualized less as a moral failing and more as a psychological condition. In Buddhism, *lobha*—often translated as craving or grasping—is one of the three root causes of suffering, alongside hatred (*dosa*) and delusion (*moha*) (Harvey 2013). These states distort perception, causing individuals to pursue satisfaction through accumulation while remaining trapped in cycles of dissatisfaction. Because craving is inherently insatiable, it cannot produce lasting fulfillment. Greed, in this view, harms not only society but the individual experiencing it, binding them to an endless loop of desire without resolution.

Even in early European language and mythology, greed is not framed as rational pursuit, but as uncontrolled hunger. The Old English linguistic roots of the word "greed" trace back to *grǣdig*, meaning ravenous or voracious (Oxford English Dictionary 2020). Mythological figures such as wolves and dragons often symbolize this insatiable appetite—creatures that consume endlessly without satisfaction (Larrington 1999). In these traditions, greed is not simply wanting—it is devouring.

Across these philosophical, religious, and cultural frameworks, the pattern is remarkably stable:

- Greed exceeds necessity
- It resists satisfaction
- It disrupts relationships and social balance

For most of human history, greed was treated as something to be restrained—ethically, socially, and spiritually.

What is historically unusual is not that greed exists.

What is unusual is that modern systems often reward it.

Greed as Symbol

Across myth and cultural narratives, greed is not only defined—it is dramatized.

It appears as:

- **the enchantment of "more"**
  (King Midas — Greek mythology)
  A king granted the power to turn everything he touches into gold, only to find that food, water, and human connection become lifeless metal (Ovid 2004).
- **the hoarded treasure that isolates its keeper**
  (Fafnir — Norse mythology)
  A man who murders for gold and transforms into a dragon, guarding his hoard in complete isolation, becoming indistinguishable from what he possesses (Larrington 1999).
- **the false god of accumulation**
  (Mammon — Biblical/Christian tradition)
  Wealth personified as an object of worship, replacing moral and relational life with devotion to material gain (Matthew 6:24; Newhauser 2000).
- **the endless hunger that never satisfies**
  (Wendigo — Algonquian folklore)
  A being consumed by insatiable hunger, often associated with greed and overconsumption, whose appetite grows the more it devours (Johnston 1995).

- **the coldness of emotional disconnection**
  (Ebenezer Scrooge — Charles Dickens, A Christmas Carol)
  A wealthy man emotionally frozen by isolation and accumulation, whose life becomes defined not by connection but by control and withholding (Dickens 1843).

These recurring images point to a deeper truth:

Greed is not just about having.
It is about becoming organized around having.

At its extreme, possession replaces identity.

The human being becomes a **human having**.

Need Is Not Greed

Human beings require resources to survive.

Food, shelter, safety, and belonging are not luxuries—they are conditions of life. Throughout history, storing resources has been a rational response to uncertainty.

Greed begins when accumulation detaches from survival.

When "enough" has already been reached—often far exceeded—and accumulation continues without limit, the logic changes. The goal is no longer security.

It becomes:

- status
- control

- insulation from vulnerability

At that point, the question shifts from:

“Do I have enough to live?”
to
“How much more can I obtain?”

This shift marks the psychological boundary where greed begins.

The Addiction Pattern

Greed follows a structure that closely resembles addiction.

In addiction, a behavior produces reward. That reward reinforces repetition. Over time, the brain adapts, and the original reward becomes insufficient. The individual requires more to achieve the same effect.

This process—known as tolerance—creates a cycle:

gain → reward → normalization → escalation

The pursuit continues not because it satisfies, but because it temporarily relieves an internal state.

Wealth and power activate reward systems tied to status, control, and recognition. These experiences can feel deeply reinforcing. But like any stimulant, their effects fade.

What once felt like success becomes baseline.
What once felt extraordinary becomes expected.

The pursuit of “more” becomes automatic.

The Psychological Layer Beneath

Addiction is not only neurological. It is often compensatory.

Many forms of compulsive behavior emerge from deeper experiences of:

- rejection
- shame
- instability
- loss of authentic self

When a person's identity is repeatedly invalidated, they may construct external sources of validation—achievement, status, accumulation—to stabilize their sense of worth.

In this sense, greed can function as:

- protection
- emotional armor
- a strategy for avoiding vulnerability

But the strategy has a limit.

Accumulation can create distance from harm, but it cannot create belonging.

When Greed Becomes Social

Most addictions are eventually recognized as destructive.

Greed is different.

It is often rewarded.

Extreme accumulation is interpreted as intelligence, discipline, or success. Wealth becomes a signal of competence. Power becomes a signal of superiority.

Under these conditions, greed becomes difficult to recognize as addiction at all.

It becomes aspiration.

And once that happens, the effects scale.

Greed no longer remains an individual behavior.
It becomes structural.

Housing becomes investment.
Healthcare becomes a market.
Work becomes extraction.

The result is a social environment shaped by:

- chronic insecurity
- competition
- and normalization of "never enough"

In such systems, entire populations are encouraged to admire the very behaviors that produce their own instability.

A Different Question

For centuries, discussions of greed have focused on morality.

Is greed wrong?
Is it sinful?
Is it unethical?

Those questions are important, but they may not be the most useful ones.

A more revealing question might be this:

What happens to a society when limitless accumulation becomes normal?

When success is defined by how much one can extract rather than how well people can live, the psychological landscape of an entire culture shifts. Cooperation weakens. Trust declines. People learn to measure themselves and others according to economic value.

Under those conditions, greed stops looking like a deviation.

It becomes the operating logic of the system.

Understanding greed as an addiction allows us to see this dynamic more clearly. It highlights how behaviors that harm collective wellbeing can nevertheless be reinforced by the structures surrounding them.

The goal of this book is not to condemn greed, but to understand the mechanism of its action, and our role as enablers of this faulty cycle.

References

Alster, Bendt. 2005. *Wisdom of Ancient Sumer*. Bethesda, MD: CDL Press.

Aquinas, Thomas. 1947. *Summa Theologica*. New York: Benziger Brothers.

Aristotle. 1999. *Nicomachean Ethics*. Translated by Terence Irwin. Indianapolis: Hackett Publishing.

Balot, Ryan K. 2001. *Greed and Injustice in Classical Athens*. Princeton, NJ: Princeton University Press.

Boyce, Mary. 2001. *Zoroastrians: Their Religious Beliefs and Practices*. London: Routledge.

Brueggemann, Walter. 2014. *Money and Possessions*. Louisville, KY: Westminster John Knox Press.

Burton, Neel. 2014. *Heaven and Hell: The Psychology of the Emotions*. Oxford: Acheron Press.

Grant, Jon E., Marc N. Potenza, Aviv Weinstein, and David A. Gorelick. 2010. "Introduction to Behavioral Addictions." *The American Journal of Drug and Alcohol Abuse* 36(5):233–241.

Harvey, Peter. 2013. *An Introduction to Buddhism: Teachings, History and Practices*. 2nd ed. Cambridge: Cambridge University Press.

Hudson, Michael. 2018. *...and Forgive Them Their Debts: Lending, Foreclosure and Redemption from Bronze Age Finance to the Jubilee Year*. Dresden: ISLET-Verlag.

Kuhrt, Amélie. 2007. *The Persian Empire: A Corpus of Sources from the Achaemenid Period.* London: Routledge.

Kuran, Timur. 2004. *Islam and Mammon: The Economic Predicaments of Islamism.* Princeton, NJ: Princeton University Press.

Larrington, Carolyne, trans. 1999. *The Poetic Edda.* Oxford: Oxford University Press.

Maté, Gabor. 2008. *In the Realm of Hungry Ghosts: Close Encounters with Addiction.* Berkeley: North Atlantic Books.

Newhauser, Richard. 2000. *The Early History of Greed: The Sin of Avarice in Early Medieval Thought and Literature.* Cambridge: Cambridge University Press.

Piketty, Thomas. 2014. *Capital in the Twenty-First Century.* Cambridge, MA: Harvard University Press.

Plato. 1992. *Republic.* Translated by G. M. A. Grube and C. D. C. Reeve. Indianapolis: Hackett Publishing.

Roth, Martha T. 1997. *Law Collections from Mesopotamia and Asia Minor.* Atlanta: Scholars Press.

Sandel, Michael J. 2012. *What Money Can't Buy: The Moral Limits of Markets.* New York: Farrar, Straus and Giroux.

Sapolsky, Robert M. 2017. *Behave: The Biology of Humans at Our Best and Worst.* New York: Penguin Press.

Singh, Nikky-Guninder Kaur. 2005. *Sikhism: An Introduction.* London: I.B. Tauris.

Volkow, Nora D., and Marisela Morales. 2015. "The Brain on Drugs: From Reward to Addiction." *Cell* 162(4):712–725.

Wilkinson, Richard, and Kate Pickett. 2009. *The Spirit Level: Why Greater Equality Makes Societies Stronger.* New York: Bloomsbury Press.

Winnicott, D. W. 1965. *The Maturational Processes and the Facilitating Environment.* New York: International Universities Press.

Oxford English Dictionary. 2020. Entry for "Greed." Oxford: Oxford University Press.

Dickens, Charles. 1843. *A Christmas Carol.* London: Chapman & Hall.

Johnston, Basil. 1995. *The Manitous: The Spiritual World of the Ojibway.* New York: HarperCollins.

Larrington, Carolyne, trans. 1999. *The Poetic Edda.* Oxford: Oxford University Press.

Newhauser, Richard. 2000. *The Early History of Greed.* Cambridge: Cambridge University Press.

Ovid. 2004. *Metamorphoses.* Translated by David Raeburn. London: Penguin Classics.

The Holy Bible, Matthew 6:24.

Chapter 2

When Greed Becomes Power

Greed alone does not reorganize society.

It can explain desire, accumulation, and excess.
But it cannot explain how entire systems come to reward, protect, and expand that accumulation.

For greed to move beyond individual behavior, it requires an instrument.

That instrument is power.

Greed and Power Are Not the Same

Greed and power are often treated as interchangeable, but they operate differently.

Greed concerns possession.
Power concerns control.

Greed seeks more.
Power secures the conditions that make "more" possible.

An individual may desire wealth, but without power, that desire remains limited. It is constrained by law, competition, and social boundaries.

Power removes those constraints.

It allows accumulation to:

- persist
- expand
- and remain protected from challenge

In this sense, greed is the drive.
Power is the structure that sustains the drive.

Power as Expansion

At small scales, greed appears as personal behavior.

At large scales, it becomes institutional.

This transition occurs when individuals or groups gain sufficient influence to shape:

- rules and laws
- markets
- access to resources

Power enables the conversion of private accumulation into public structure.

Wealth becomes leverage.
Leverage becomes influence.
Influence becomes policy.

Over time, systems begin to reflect the interests of those who hold the most resources (Piketty 2014).

Those with more resources have greater capacity to:

- invest
- influence
- and defend their position

As a result, accumulation becomes self-reinforcing.

Power as Protection

Power does not only expand greed.

It protects it.

In most forms of addiction, external limits eventually intervene—legal, social, or physical.

Greed operates differently because it often aligns with systems of reward.

Extreme accumulation is not typically punished.
It is often legitimized.

Wealth is framed as:

- intelligence
- discipline
- success

Power strengthens this framing.

Institutions—from markets to political systems—frequently normalize outcomes that would otherwise be questioned (Sandel 2012).

Under these conditions, behaviors that concentrate resources at the top are not experienced as violations.

They are experienced as achievements.

Power as Normalization

Perhaps the most significant function of power is not expansion or protection, but normalization.

Power shapes perception.

It defines what appears reasonable, desirable, or inevitable.

When systems consistently reward accumulation, people begin to internalize it as a measure of worth.

Over time:

- inequality becomes expected
- competition becomes naturalized
- scarcity becomes assumed

In such environments, greed is no longer recognized as a problem.

It becomes aspiration.

This is the point at which greed transitions fully into system.

This process aligns with broader sociological analyses of how norms and institutions shape behavior and belief (Foucault 1977).

From Behavior to System

Once normalized, greed no longer depends on individual intent.

It becomes embedded in structure.

Markets reward growth over sufficiency.
Institutions prioritize efficiency over care.
Work organizes around productivity rather than sustainability.

Individuals operating within these systems may not consciously identify as greedy.

They are simply responding to incentives.

Yet the outcome remains the same:

Accumulation without limit, scaled across society.

A Structural Loop

At this stage, a feedback loop emerges:

- accumulation increases influence
- influence reshapes systems
- systems reward further accumulation

The cycle reinforces itself.

Breaking it becomes difficult, not because individuals lack awareness, but because the structure itself sustains the pattern.

Empirical research on inequality and social outcomes shows how concentrated wealth reshapes life conditions across entire populations (Wilkinson and Pickett 2009).

Toward the Inner Layer

Understanding power explains how greed becomes system.

But it does not yet explain why individuals become attached to accumulation in the first place.

Why does "more" feel necessary?
Why does loss feel threatening?
Why does control become emotionally significant?

To answer these questions, we need to look beneath behavior and structure.

We need to look at the psychological layer.

References

Foucault, Michel. 1977. *Discipline and Punish: The Birth of the Prison*. New York: Pantheon Books.

Piketty, Thomas. 2014. *Capital in the Twenty-First Century*. Cambridge, MA: Harvard University Press.

Sandel, Michael J. 2012. *What Money Can't Buy: The Moral Limits of Markets*. New York: Farrar, Straus and Giroux.

Wilkinson, Richard, and Kate Pickett. 2009. *The Spirit Level: Why Greater Equality Makes Societies Stronger*. New York: Bloomsbury Press.

CHAPTER 3

The Neurology of "Never Enough

If greed were only an idea, it would be easier to interrupt.

If it were only a philosophy, a person could simply reason their way out of it.

But the experience of "never enough" does not live only in thought. It lives in the body. It lives in circuits of reward, anticipation, stress, comparison, and threat. It is part of our biology. By the time greed becomes visible in behavior, it is often already supported by a nervous system trained to regulate by using external control (Volkow and Morales 2015).

The modern world often talks about greed as if it were a conscious choice made by unusually selfish people. Neuroscience suggests a more complex picture. Repeated pursuit of reward can gradually reshape motivation itself. In addiction research, the core issue is not simply pleasure but the transformation of wanting into a chronic state of pursuit that no longer produces genuine satisfaction. The person keeps chasing the reward not because it feels deeply fulfilling, but because the neural systems driving motivation have become sensitized (Berridge and Robinson 2016).

This distinction between **wanting and liking** is crucial for understanding greed.

This section does not attempt to reduce greed to brain chemistry. Rather, it shows how patterns of accumulation, once established, can become reinforced at the level of the nervous system, making them difficult to interrupt.

Dopamine Is Not Happiness

Popular culture often describes dopamine as the "pleasure chemical," but this is misleading. Dopamine plays a much broader role in learning, motivation, salience detection, and goal-directed behavior. It helps the brain identify what might matter and energize action toward those goals (Schultz 2016).

Dopamine neurons respond strongly to **reward prediction error**, the gap between what we expected and what we actually received. When outcomes exceed expectations, dopamine signals reinforce the behavior that produced them, increasing the likelihood that the same behavior will be repeated (Schultz 2016).

Wealth and power therefore function not only as resources but also as powerful signals. They signal status, security, influence, and future opportunity. Each gain teaches the nervous system that these outcomes are important and worth pursuing again.

But dopamine does not produce contentment.

Research shows that the neural systems that generate **desire** are partly separate from those that generate **pleasure**. A person can therefore want something intensely without necessarily enjoying it once it is obtained (Berridge and Robinson 2016).

This distinction helps explain why accumulation can escalate even when satisfaction does not.

The Brain Learns to Chase Cues and Reaches Tolerance

Addiction does not depend only on the reward itself; it also depends on the signals that predict it. Casinos, for example, do not rely solely on monetary gain. They are structured around lights, sounds, near-misses, and anticipation. Social media platforms operate in similar ways, reinforcing behavior through notifications, intermittent rewards, and the promise of social recognition. In both cases, the cues surrounding the reward gradually become powerful motivators in their own right.

Neuroscientific research suggests that repeated exposure to rewards can sensitize the brain to these signals. According to incentive-sensitization theory, cues associated with reward begin to capture attention, activate desire, and narrow behavioral focus even before the reward itself is obtained (Berridge and Robinson 2016). The nervous system becomes organized around anticipation. The body generates a strong motivational signal to pursue the reward, and the mind often interprets this internal activation as evidence that the goal must be important.

Over time, another process emerges: **tolerance**. One of the defining characteristics of addiction is that what once produced a powerful response gradually becomes normal. The brain recalibrates its baseline, and larger or more frequent rewards are required to produce the same psychological effect (Koob and Le Moal 2001). In substance addiction this may involve increasing doses. In behavioral addictions it may involve escalating risks or intensifying engagement.

In the pursuit of wealth or status, tolerance can manifest as a shifting definition of abundance. Achievements that once symbolized success may come to feel ordinary or insufficient as expectations adjust. The threshold of "enough" moves continually forward. As the brain adapts to escalation, limits can begin to feel threatening. Redistribution may be experienced as loss, and equality as deprivation.

In this sense, greed is not simply the possession of wealth but a form of chronic motivational dysregulation in which the brain becomes trained to pursue ever-greater rewards without reaching stable satisfaction.

If Dopamine Drives Wanting, What Produces Contentment?

Dopamine plays a powerful role in motivation and pursuit, but it is not the chemical basis of satisfaction. Dopamine prepares the organism to act—to seek, to explore, to obtain. It is fundamentally a system of **anticipation** rather than completion (Schultz 2016).

Contentment arises from different neural processes.

Instead of activating circuits of pursuit, contentment is associated with systems that regulate **safety, social connection, and emotional balance**.

Several biological mechanisms are particularly important.

Serotonin and Emotional Stability:

Serotonin plays a central role in regulating mood, emotional stability, and impulse control. While dopamine encourages action toward potential rewards, serotonin is often associated with a sense of **sufficiency and calm regulation**.

Research suggests that serotonin helps stabilize behavior by reducing impulsivity and supporting long-term regulation rather than immediate pursuit (Carhart-Harris and Nutt 2017).

In this sense, serotonin contributes to the experience of feeling **settled rather than driven**.

Oxytocin and Social Connection:

Another important contributor to contentment is oxytocin, a neuropeptide strongly associated with bonding, trust, and social attachment.

Humans evolved as intensely social organisms. Experiences of connection—caregiving, friendship, intimacy, cooperation—activate oxytocin systems that help produce feelings of safety and belonging (Carter 2014).

These experiences can generate a form of satisfaction fundamentally different from reward pursuit. Rather than stimulating excitement, they create **warmth and emotional security**.

The Parasympathetic Nervous System:

Contentment is also closely related to the balance of the autonomic nervous system.

When individuals feel safe and secure, the **parasympathetic nervous system** becomes more active. Heart rate slows, breathing deepens, and the body shifts into states associated with restoration and regulation (Porges 2011).

This physiological state supports feelings of calm, safety, and emotional balance—conditions that make the experience of "enough" possible.

Meaning and Coherence:

Beyond neurochemistry, contentment is also linked to the brain's ability to integrate experiences into a coherent sense of **meaning**.

Research in psychology consistently shows that individuals who experience **purpose**, **belonging**, and **social trust** report higher levels of life satisfaction than those who focus primarily on external rewards (Diener, Oishi, and Tay 2018).

Meaning does not activate the same pursuit circuits as reward. Instead, it stabilizes attention and emotion around **relationships, contribution**, and **identity**.

The Conflict Between Pursuit and Contentment

Understanding these systems helps explain an important paradox.

The biological systems that produce excitement and pursuit are not the same systems that produce calm and satisfaction.

Dopamine drives movement toward goals.
Serotonin and parasympathetic regulation support stability and

emotional balance.
Oxytocin supports connection and belonging.

When cultures continuously stimulate pursuit—through competition, status comparison, and economic escalation—they amplify the dopamine-driven system of **wanting**.

But the conditions that support contentment—security, belonging, stability, and meaningful connection—may remain underdeveloped.

Under those circumstances, individuals can experience intense motivation and success while still feeling that something is missing.

The nervous system continues to chase stimulation even when the deeper conditions for contentment have not been met.

Social Comparison and Hierarchy

Human beings are not reward-seeking in isolation. Our brains constantly evaluate relative position within social hierarchies.

Research in social neuroscience shows that reward systems respond not only to what individuals receive but also to how their outcomes compare with those of others (Fliessbach et al. 2007). Gaining more than others can activate reward circuits, while receiving less can trigger feelings of distress and threat.

The brain therefore does not simply ask:

Did I gain?

It also asks:

Did I gain **more than them**?

When status itself becomes rewarding, accumulation becomes a way of stabilizing position within a competitive hierarchy. Status and dominance are associated with measurable changes in dopaminergic activity and motivational systems (Sapolsky 2005).

This means greed is not fueled solely by need. It is fueled by **comparison**.

In societies structured around competition and ranking, the experience of insufficiency can become nearly universal, because there will always be someone who possesses more.

Stress and the Biology of Scarcity

Reward is only half the story. Stress is the other half.

Addiction research increasingly describes long-term compulsive behavior as a shift from pleasure seeking to relief seeking. Over time, repeated stimulation of reward systems recruits stress and anti-reward systems in the brain. The person continues the behavior not to achieve pleasure but to escape the discomfort of withdrawal and dysregulation (Koob and Le Moal 2001).

Chronic stress can therefore deepen cycles of compulsive pursuit.

Research on scarcity and economic precarity shows that unstable conditions narrow attention, increase cognitive load, and bias decision-making toward short-term solutions (Mullainathan and

Shafir 2013). Under conditions of insecurity, accumulation can appear to promise safety.

More money, more status, more credentials, more protection.

Yet when stress systems remain chronically activated, the sense of security rarely stabilizes.

The individual does not reach calm; they reach temporary relief.

Trauma and the Rejected Self

The neurology of "never enough" is also shaped by personal history.

Research on childhood adversity shows that trauma, neglect, bullying, and chronic rejection can produce lasting changes in stress regulation and emotional processing (Teicher and Samson 2016). These experiences can increase vulnerability to compulsive behavior and addiction later in life.

Addiction is therefore often less about pleasure than about compensation.

When a person's authentic emotional self is repeatedly rejected or invalidated, the individual may construct a protective identity organized around performance, achievement, or control. Winnicott's concept of the **false self** describes this adaptation: a defensive outer personality that protects a vulnerable inner self from further injury (Winnicott 1965).

The individual may achieve extraordinary success while internally remaining organized around avoidance of rejection.

They may be admired, yet feel unseen.

They may be surrounded by people, yet remain profoundly alone.

Rejection and Social Pain

Social rejection is not trivial to the brain. Neuroscience research demonstrates overlap between the neural systems involved in physical pain and those activated during experiences of social exclusion (Eisenberger and Lieberman 2004).

From an evolutionary perspective, this makes sense. For most of human history, survival depended on belonging to a group. Exclusion from the group could be life-threatening.

When authenticity becomes associated with rejection, individuals may adopt strategies designed to reduce exposure to social pain. These strategies may include masking, performance, dominance, or relentless achievement.

Greed can become fused with identity not only because people want more, but because accumulation appears to reduce vulnerability.

But insulation is not the same as belonging.

Why "More" Never Resolves the Void

The pattern begins to reveal itself.

Dopamine encourages pursuit. Cues gain motivational power. Baselines shift through tolerance. Social comparison intensifies striving. Stress narrows attention. Trauma magnifies the need for control. Shame drives compensatory identity construction.

These processes can trap individuals in a loop where expansion feels necessary.

Yet the nervous system continues to encounter the same problem:

More stimulation does not create enoughness.

Enoughness is not merely a quantity. It is a regulatory state supported by safety, attachment, meaning, and social connection.

A person can possess extraordinary resources and still experience themselves as deficient.

In this state, abundance does not feel abundant.

It feels temporarily defended.

A Society Built on Neural Vulnerabilities

This chapter does not excuse greed. Rather, it helps explain why the feeling of "never enough" can be so difficult to interrupt once it becomes embedded not only in individual nervous systems but also in the structures of society itself. Surprisingly, the experience of "never enough" is not only a physiological state shaped by reward systems in the brain; it is also a widespread psychological condition produced by the environments in which many people now live.

In systems organized around constant comparison, competition, and performance, the sense of insufficiency becomes normalized. Many individuals begin to experience a persistent background feeling that they are behind, lacking, or not yet adequate. Within such environments, patterns of chronic stress and relational insecurity can accumulate over time. What I have described in my earlier work as **Compounded Relational c-PTSD (CRC-PTSD)** can emerge as the psychological outcome of systems that repeatedly expose individuals to evaluation, rejection, instability, and institutional indifference.

A striking paradox appears within this dynamic. Not only do societies increasingly normalize forms of behavior that resemble addiction, they also celebrate them. Endless productivity, constant optimization, self-surveillance, and the relentless pursuit of wealth or recognition are often framed as signs of ambition or excellence. Yet the same system that glorifies these pursuits simultaneously produces widespread feelings of inadequacy and exhaustion.

In this sense, the system monetizes insecurity. Industries of self-improvement, productivity, and personal optimization flourish by promising relief from the very pressures the system helps generate. Individuals are encouraged to continuously refine themselves—improving their bodies, careers, credentials, and personal brands—yet the standard of adequacy continues to move. The result is a cycle in which people increasingly treat themselves as projects to be optimized, or even as products to be developed and marketed.

Modern economic systems therefore do not operate solely through rational calculation. They interact continuously with predictable features of human neurobiology: reward learning, social comparison, stress regulation, and fear of exclusion. When these mechanisms are repeatedly stimulated, the pursuit of more becomes self-reinforcing.

A culture organized in this way gradually teaches individuals to measure their worth through accumulation, to equate status with security, and to interpret expansion as evidence of personal value, while accumulation will never create the sense of satisfaction, calm and safety humans pursue naturally.

Under such conditions, greed no longer appears as a deviation from the system.

It becomes the system's operating logic.

Understanding the neurology of "never enough" therefore reveals something important. The pursuit of limitless accumulation is not simply a moral problem or a matter of individual character.

It is a **biological and social feedback loop**. An Echo chamber made out of human insecurity and fears.

And within that loop, behaviors that resemble addiction can easily come to look like success.

References

Berridge, Kent C., and Terry E. Robinson. 2016. "Liking, Wanting, and the Incentive-Sensitization Theory of Addiction." *American Psychologist* 71(8):670–679.

Carhart-Harris, Robin L., and David J. Nutt. 2017. "Serotonin and Brain Function." *Neuropharmacology* 142:101–113.

Carter, C. Sue. 2014. "Oxytocin Pathways and the Evolution of Human Behavior." *Annual Review of Psychology* 65:17–39.

Diener, Ed, Shigehiro Oishi, and Louis Tay. 2018. "Advances in Subjective Well-Being Research." *Nature Human Behaviour* 2:253–260.

Eisenberger, Naomi I., and Matthew D. Lieberman. 2004. "Why Rejection Hurts: A Common Neural Alarm System for Physical and Social Pain." *Trends in Cognitive Sciences* 8(7):294–300.

Fliessbach, Klaus, Thomas Weber, Peter Trautner, Christian Dohmen, Uwe Sunde, Christian Elger, and Armin Falk. 2007. "Social Comparison Affects Reward-Related Brain Activity." *Science* 318(5854):1305–1308.

Koob, George F., and Michel Le Moal. 2001. "Drug Addiction, Dysregulation of Reward, and Allostasis." *Neuropsychopharmacology* 24(2):97–129.

Mullainathan, Sendhil, and Eldar Shafir. 2013. *Scarcity: Why Having Too Little Means So Much*. New York: Times Books.

Porges, Stephen W. 2011. *The Polyvagal Theory: Neurophysiological Foundations of Emotions, Attachment, Communication, and Self-Regulation*. New York: W. W. Norton.

Sapolsky, Robert M. 2005. "The Influence of Social Hierarchy on Primate Health." *Science* 308(5722):648–652.

Schultz, Wolfram. 2016. "Dopamine Reward Prediction Error Coding." *Dialogues in Clinical Neuroscience* 18(1):23–32.

Teicher, Martin H., and Jacqueline A. Samson. 2016. "Annual Research Review: Enduring Neurobiological Effects of Childhood

Abuse and Neglect." *Journal of Child Psychology and Psychiatry* 57(3):241–266.

Volkow, Nora D., and Marisela Morales. 2015. "The Brain on Drugs: From Reward to Addiction." *Cell* 162(4):712–725.

Winnicott, D. W. 1965. *The Maturational Processes and the Facilitating Environment.* New York: International Universities Press.

PART II

THE PSYCHOLOGY OF GREED-ADDICTION

Chapter 4

The Fragile Core: Greed as a Coping Mechanism

In our culture, greed is often interpreted as confidence.

From the outside, individuals who accumulate extreme wealth or power can appear decisive, ambitious, and self-assured. Their actions suggest certainty and control. They dominate industries, command institutions, and shape the lives of millions of people. Success at this scale is often interpreted as evidence of psychological strength.

But the psychology underlying relentless accumulation may tell a different story.

In many cases, the pursuit of endless expansion does not emerge from a stable sense of self but from its absence. Beneath the drive for recognition, control, and superiority there may exist something far more fragile: a deep vulnerability organized around shame, insecurity, and the fear of being insignificant.

The pursuit of more can therefore function as a psychological defense.

The Wound Beneath the Armor, and the Manufactured Mask

Human identity does not develop in isolation. It forms inside relationships. In early life, caregivers function as mirrors: not in a sentimental sense, but in a developmental one. The infant's nervous system cannot fully name, organize, or regulate its internal states alone. A caregiver's attunement—accurate emotional recognition, soothing, protection, and repair—reflects the child back to themselves until the child can carry that mirror internally (Bowlby 1969; Ainsworth, Blehar, Waters, and Wall 1978; Siegel 1999). This is how a stable sense of self forms: a body that learns "my feelings make sense," "my needs are allowed," and "I can be distressed and still remain connected."

When that mirroring is consistent, a person tends to develop a basic, embodied worth that is not completely dependent on external validation. They may still want approval—humans are social—but they are not organized around it.

But when early environments involve rejection, humiliation, neglect, bullying, or chronic comparison, the mirror does something else. It distorts. The child learns that certain emotions are "too much," that needs burden others, that authenticity is punished, and that belonging is conditional. The developing self may not feel safe enough to exist openly.

Winnicott gave this adaptation a precise name: the false self—an externally oriented self built to maintain attachment and reduce danger when the true self cannot be safely expressed (Winnicott 1965). The false self is often highly competent: productive, impressive, socially successful. It can look like strength. But it remains fragile because it is stabilizing identity through performance rather than through being real. Its stability depends on continued approval, continued achievement, continued control.

In modern life, this is no longer merely a childhood phenomenon. In a world structured by manufactured scarcity and the glorification of greed, the false self becomes an adult requirement. We are often forced by survival to mask: to perform competence, to hide vulnerability, to compress our humanity into what institutions will tolerate. People learn quickly that authenticity can cost employment, social standing, access to care, or safety. In that environment, developing a true self is not just hard; it can feel impractical. The cumulative psychic injury of repeated relational harms across institutions—schools, workplaces, bureaucracies, social hierarchies—that do not merely stress people, but repeatedly deny their reality, demand compliance, and reward self-erasure.

What makes CRC-PTSD so corrosive is that it doesn't only create symptoms. It trains identity. It trains a person to become legible to power rather than true to self. Over time, relational wounds stop feeling like exceptions and start feeling like the conditions of adulthood. The person learns to treat self-suppression as maturity.

Then something subtle and devastating happens: the armor gets mistaken for the self.

This confusion produces chronic disconnection. When you have not been mirrored accurately—when your needs were repeatedly treated as burdensome—you may reach adulthood without a reliable inner language for your real needs, especially your need for authenticity and co-regulation. The true self becomes the shamed self: the goofy, careless, tender, imaginative part that could expand beyond your own expectations, but that was trained into hiding. Under perfectionism, productivity culture, and scarcity logic, that part is not just rejected—it is made to feel irresponsible and taboo.

So you only remember your whole self in rare moments of genuine connection, when another person's presence briefly allows your nervous system to soften. And if those moments are rare, the true self begins to feel like a myth. You forget it exists.

When the true self becomes inaccessible, life loses meaning. And meaning is not a luxury—it is a stabilizer. Without it, the nervous system often shifts into high alert, scanning for control. At that point accumulation starts to look like safety. This is the psychological bridge between trauma and greed: control becomes the substitute for belonging.

At first, accumulation works. It produces relief. It creates leverage. It reduces exposure. The person feels less dependent, less rejectable, less at the mercy of others. This is why greed can look like strength while functioning like regulation: it dampens shame and uncertainty for a moment. But like any addiction, it reaches a plateau. The brain adapts; the relief shortens; the comparison returns; the fear returns; the pursuit escalates (Koob and Le Moal 2001; Berridge and Robinson 2016). The person becomes functional inside the strategy, not healed beyond it.

Pulling from my own experience of a behavioral addiction, I'm going to compare Greed with an Eating disorder to illustrate the addiction mechanism of action. Anorexia often begins as a pursuit of control and safety through thinness. It is not primarily vanity; it is frequently a regulation strategy for helplessness, fear, and identity confusion. The person becomes increasingly "successful" at weight loss strategies while becoming increasingly disconnected from the body's needs and from meaning. Even near death, the illness can be defended because it feels like the only stable form of control (Bruch 1973; Treasure, Claudino, and Zucker 2010; Fairburn 2008). For an Anorexic patient losing any amount of weight won't be enough and it usually decreases to a lower number after every weight loss achievement. In other words the only low enough weight is when the patient is dead. Greed addiction shares that structure: control pursued as safety, satisfaction plateauing, reality narrowing, and comparison becoming endless. The crucial difference is that greed often remains socially applauded. The person still "functions." They still win. And because they win, no one intervenes—while the void persists.

And the void persists for one central reason: **the original wound was relational. It cannot be healed by a non-relational substitute.**

This is the part that makes greed uniquely tragic. If someone becomes a mask of wealth, power, beauty, productivity—then even if others genuinely love them, they cannot fully trust it. Not only because others may be reacting to the mask, but because the person cannot trust themselves and to drop the mask around others. Deep down, they know they have not allowed anyone to meet their real self. Love feels unconfirmable. Admiration is loud, but it is not mirroring.

The Addiction Pattern

The addiction cycle repeats:

gain → reward → normalization → escalation

Over time, the pursuit of "more" becomes automatic.

Eventually, another painful cycle emerges. The individual may feel a profound longing for closeness and genuine connection, yet they struggle to trust that anyone truly wants them for who they are. At this point, the behavior is no longer driven primarily by satisfaction. Instead, it becomes an attempt to prevent the discomfort of losing control, status, or validation.

The pursuit of accumulation becomes less about pleasure and more about avoiding emptiness.

When this pattern stabilizes, the boundary between ambition and addiction begins to blur.

And here is where the cultural story does its deepest damage: people are indoctrinated early that the world is a jungle, that "all is fair in love and war," that cruelty is realism and compassion is naïve. Those phrases often function as anesthesia for cognitive dissonance. They allow people to harm others while still imagining themselves as good. Over time, the dissonance between what the heart knows it needs—connection, safety, mutual care—and what the system rewards—extraction, dominance, hoarding—can disappear not because the heart stopped knowing, but because identity fused with the mask. This is how a society can become full of "successful" people who are profoundly disconnected from their real needs, and therefore profoundly disconnected from the needs of others.

At the deepest level, what greed addiction protects is not strength. It protects fragility from being seen.

What healing actually is (and what the end goal is)

Healing is not becoming more impressive. Healing is regaining the capacity to feel safe without the mask.

That means the goal is not to destroy the false self—because it once protected you. The goal is to outgrow the necessity of it.

The nervous system learns safety through repeated experiences of being real and remaining connected. This is why healing is relational. The "wound beneath the armor" formed in an environment where authenticity cost you connection. Healing requires environments where authenticity creates connection. That is the corrective experience.

Practically, this means three interlocking shifts:

Restoring inner mirroring: learning to recognize your own states and needs without contempt—especially the tender ones you were trained to shame. This is the rebuilding of the internal caregiver, the internal witness (Siegel 1999; Gilbert 2009). I will write a book on the topic of reparenting self in the future.

Restoring relational safety: experiences of co-regulation—being with people who can hold your nervous system without requiring performance. This is not dependence; it is the developmental condition humans need to become secure (Bowlby 1969; Porges 2011).

Restoring meaning beyond comparison: withdrawing worth from the marketplace and returning it to personhood—so that being alive is not something you must earn.

When these conditions strengthen, the need for control through accumulation weakens—not because you forced it to, but because the nervous system no longer needs that substitute.

That is the deepest reversal: the day you can be unmasked and still feel safe.

That is healing. Easier said than done!

Narcissism and the Fear of Insignificance

Psychological research on narcissism helps clarify why greed can escalate beyond any rational need. Narcissism is often caricatured as vanity or arrogance, but many scholars emphasize that grandiosity frequently functions as a protective structure built around a fragile self—an attempt to defend against shame, insecurity, and a persistent fear of being insignificant (Pincus and Lukowitsky 2010).

In this framework, grandiosity is less a sign of genuine self-confidence than a *strategy of stabilization*. The individual constructs an identity organized around superiority: being exceptional, being above, being untouchable. Status, admiration, and visible success become the external mirrors that temporarily confirm worth. Recognition provides a brief sense of relief—proof that the self is real, safe, and important.

Common Narcissistic Coping Strategies

(Ways the fragile self tries to stabilize itself and greed is one of them)

Let's take a look at some of the most common coping patterns described in clinical and social-psychological literature. People can use more than one, and the same person may shift strategies depending on context.

1) Grandiosity and superiority

Maintaining self-worth through being "above": smarter, better, exceptional, untouchable.

2) Validation-seeking and admiration dependence

Needing constant praise, attention, "proof" of worth; distress when admiration drops.

3) Status signaling

Using visible markers—titles, brands, aesthetics, proximity to prestige—to stabilize identity.

4) Entitlement

Believing normal limits don't apply; interpreting needs as rights; resentment when others say no.

5) Devaluation

Protecting the self by diminishing others: "they're stupid," "they're inferior," "they don't matter."

6) Control and micromanagement

Regulating insecurity through domination of environment, people, narratives, outcomes.

7) Image management / persona construction

Living through a curated self; prioritizing appearance over inner truth; fear of exposure.

8) Blame-shifting and externalization

When shame arises, it's moved outward: others are at fault; the system made me do it; "you're too sensitive."

9) Rage and retaliation (narcissistic injury response)

When the self-image is threatened: disproportionate anger, punishment, revenge, or humiliation of the challenger.

10) Gaslighting and reality control

Maintaining dominance by destabilizing others' perception; rewriting events; denying harm.

11) Triangulation

Using third parties to maintain power: creating alliances, turning people against each other, dividing groups.

12) Victimhood as control

Presenting as persecuted or misunderstood to avoid accountability and regain moral superiority.

13) Extraction in relationships

Using people as functions: attention, labor, sex, status, emotional service—rather than mutuality.

14) Discarding

Ending relationships abruptly when someone becomes inconvenient, too demanding, or no longer supplies validation.

15) Greed / hoarding / accumulation

One pathway among many: insulating the self through money, assets, influence, and "unlosable" leverage.

Greed, as I'm using it in this book, is a **coping strategy**: a specific behavioral route the nervous system takes when it doesn't feel safe. The implicit belief is, "If I can accumulate enough—money, property, status, leverage—I won't be vulnerable anymore." In that sense, greed is not only desire; it is an attempt to regulate fear, shame, and dependency through external control. It can escalate even when needs are met because what it is trying to solve is not need—it is threat.

Narcissism, by contrast, is a **coping system**: an entire psychological organization designed to prevent certain internal states—especially shame, insignificance, and helplessness—from being felt. Because it is a system, it can deploy many different strategies to stabilize the self-image. Greed is one possible tool in that defensive toolkit, especially in cultures that reward accumulation, but it is not the only one.

This distinction matters because it clarifies the path to healing. If greed is a strategy, it can loosen when people develop other ways to feel safe—ways rooted in regulation, connection, and meaning. If narcissism is a system, the work goes deeper: learning to tolerate ordinary vulnerability without collapse, rebuilding a true self that doesn't require performance, and creating relational environments where authenticity can exist without punishment. The end goal in both cases is the same: **the ability to feel safe without the mask.**

A Fragile Foundation

Understanding the fragile core beneath greed addiction does not excuse harmful behavior. But it helps explain why some individuals may pursue wealth, recognition, and power long after practical needs have been satisfied, and at the expense of harming others.

The drive for more may be rooted not only in ambition but in an unresolved attempt to stabilize a self that never learned to feel safe without an attuned and caring external source of safety.

In such cases, accumulation becomes an emotional strategy.

The world sees power.

The individual experiences protection.

But protection is not the same as peace. Psychological safety is as vital as our basic physical needs and without it, survival becomes increasingly harder to achieve. When we can't learn to create safety for our psyche, we start having physical illnesses that can't be easily explained by physiology alone.

References

Ainsworth, Mary D. S., Mary C. Blehar, Everett Waters, and Sally Wall. 1978. *Patterns of Attachment: A Psychological Study of the Strange Situation*. Hillsdale, NJ: Lawrence Erlbaum.

Berridge, Kent C., and Terry E. Robinson. 2016. "Liking, Wanting, and the Incentive-Sensitization Theory of Addiction." *American Psychologist* 71(8):670–679.

Bowlby, John. 1969. *Attachment and Loss: Volume 1. Attachment*. New York: Basic Books.

Bruch, Hilde. 1973. *Eating Disorders: Obesity, Anorexia Nervosa, and the Person Within*. New York: Basic Books.

Fairburn, Christopher G. 2008. *Cognitive Behavior Therapy and Eating Disorders*. New York: Guilford Press.

Gilbert, Paul. 2009. *The Compassionate Mind*. London: Constable.

Koob, George F., and Michel Le Moal. 2001. "Drug Addiction, Dysregulation of Reward, and Allostasis." *Neuropsychopharmacology* 24(2):97–129.

Pincus, Aaron L., and Mark R. Lukowitsky. 2010. "Pathological Narcissism and Narcissistic Personality Disorder." *Annual Review of Clinical Psychology* 6:421–446.

Porges, Stephen W. 2011. *The Polyvagal Theory: Neurophysiological Foundations of Emotions, Attachment, Communication, and Self-Regulation*. New York: W. W. Norton.

Siegel, Daniel J. 1999. *The Developing Mind: How Relationships and the Brain Interact to Shape Who We Are.* New York: Guilford Press.

Treasure, Janet, A. M. Claudino, and Nancy Zucker. 2010. "Eating Disorders." *The Lancet* 375(9714):583–593.

Winnicott, D. W. 1965. *The Maturational Processes and the Facilitating Environment.* New York: International Universities Press.

CHAPTER 5

Emotional Numbing and The Mask of Success

Emotional numbing is often misunderstood as the absence of feeling. It is not. It is the nervous system's decision—often an intelligent one—that feeling everything would be unbearable. When the world repeatedly proves unsafe, the psyche does not simply "cope." It reorganizes. It reduces range. It narrows attention. It turns down the volume on grief, tenderness, outrage, wonder, and even love and trust. The cost is that once the knob is turned down, it also turns down the beauty of life—beauty that can only be felt through slowness and presence. The over working to maintain the mask dulls compassion and interrupts the very conditions that make genuine connection possible: being seen and being able to see others at the same time.

In the world shaped by greed addiction, emotional numbing appears on both sides of the hierarchy.

It appears in those who accumulate—because to extract without conscience requires disconnection. And it appears in those who live beneath extraction—because chronic precarity and institutional dismissal produce the same protective shutdown. In both cases, numbness functions as an adaptation to an environment where full humanity is costly.

This chapter is about how that numbness becomes a **mask**—and how that mask can look like "success" for a few and a "rat wheel" for most.

Two Nervous Systems, One Strategy

For the greed-addicted, numbness is often a prerequisite for power. To profit from suffering without collapsing under it, the person must convert other people's pain into abstraction: numbers, "efficiency," "market realities," "collateral damage," "acceptable losses." Distance becomes a professional skill. Emotional detachment becomes competence. The more the person rises, the easier it becomes to avoid mirrors—to avoid anyone who can reflect what their choices are doing to human beings.

For those harmed by greed—those living with CRC-PTSD—numbness is usually not chosen. It is induced. It grows out of repeated experiences of being evaluated, dismissed, delayed, denied, or treated as a problem to manage. Over time, the body learns that hope is dangerous because hope leads to disappointment; that protest is dangerous because protest leads to punishment; that softness is dangerous because softness attracts exploitation. In trauma psychology, this often appears as shutdown, dissociation, emotional flattening, and a kind of "functional survival" (Herman 1992; van der Kolk 2014).

A violent system can also manufacture numbness through complicity. When survival depends on serving the priorities of the powerful, people are routinely placed in roles where following orders requires participating in harm—enforcing policies, denying care, extracting labor, or reproducing scarcity. If working for the successful and the wealthy becomes the only path to stability, and emotional detachment is relabeled as "professionalism," many people learn to dissociate from the pain they are helping to cause.

Otherwise the cognitive dissonance—knowing what is wrong while continuing to do it to survive—can quietly corrode the soul.

So we end up with a society in which the powerful numb themselves to keep extracting and the harmed numb themselves to keep following orders to survive. Different positions, similar protective outcome.

The Mask of Success

Modern culture is remarkably effective at moral inversion—at turning the story in front of our eyes until people stop recognizing what they are looking at.

It teaches the population to admire what is actually wounding them.

It teaches us to call restraint "discipline" even when it is self-erasure. It teaches us to call overwork "ambition" even when it is an addiction. It teaches us to call emotional disconnection "strength" even when it is fear.

This inversion is not accidental. It is structurally useful.

When people believe the mask is the self, they will invest their lives in perfecting the mask.

And that is highly profitable but does not satisfy the requirement for feeling loved and safe.

Making Beautiful Ugly and Ugly Beautiful

One of the clearest examples is the aestheticization of starvation.

A starving body became a standard. A thinness that signals depletion became the cultural symbol of desirability. We watched—almost casually—as girls learned to suffocate themselves into a narrative of femininity that requires shrinking, pleasing, and disappearing. The body became a site of moral performance: hunger as virtue, deprivation as proof, self-denial as status.

Clinically, eating disorders often function as control strategies under conditions of helplessness and fear—attempts to regulate chaos through the body (Bruch 1973; Fairburn 2008). But culturally, the "discipline" of starvation was repackaged as beauty. Suffering was reframed as aesthetic achievement.

This is the mask of success at the level of the body.

And it is not only about beauty. It is about legibility. It is about being accepted as "the right kind" of girl, the right kind of woman, the right kind of body—within a scarcity culture where attention and safety feel limited.

Under patriarchy and commodified femininity, women are often socialized to treat their bodies as projects for public evaluation rather than as homes for lived experience (Wolf 1991; Bordo 1993). When the market colonizes the body, the body stops being a self and becomes an advertisement. And the advertisement must compete.

Here is the deeper link to greed addiction: the same structure that trains the wealthy to accumulate trains the rest to self-edit. Both are organized around comparison. Both are organized around "never enough." One hoards externally; the other often hoards internally—hoarding perfection, self-control, and approval as substitutes for safety.

CRC-PTSD and the Performative Self

CRC-PTSD, is not merely "stress." It is compounded relational injury: repeated harm from people and institutions, repeated experiences of invisibility, disbelief, and conditional belonging. In such an environment, the self becomes strategic. People learn to perform stability, competence, politeness, and gratitude because those performances are often prerequisites for survival.

This is not "authentic professionalism." It is coerced legibility.

It creates a chronic conflict: the inner world becomes more and more real, trauma stacks, braids, and echoes louder each time, but is less and less shareable. The person learns to be emotionally flat in public. Over time, the mask becomes habitual and one forgets how to feel and be human. The nervous system stops offering the full range of signals because those signals were repeatedly punished, and the cognitive dissonance is exhausting.

The result is numbness as survival.

But it comes with a cost: when the body cannot express need, the self cannot be fully known—by others or by oneself. Meaning thins. Desire becomes confusing. The person can still function, but functioning is not the same as living. The person functions more like an engine, a robot, a machine rather than a human with a full range of emotions, and inner wisdom. Because once we stop fully knowing ourselves and respecting our needs, we simply forget why we live. Not to be happy, but to grow and learn and make it better for everyone and the generations to come.

Greed, Gender, and the Policing of Identity

The logic of the mask is also gendered.

Patriarchal systems do not merely "prefer" certain gender expressions; they enforce legibility. They train people into narrow roles because narrow roles are easier to control. Historically, modern institutions have often treated gender as a binary classification tied to discipline, labor organization, and social order—while gender diversity has existed across cultures and historical periods far beyond that binary (Butler 1990; Fausto-Sterling 2000).

This matters because one of the deepest forms of relational trauma is being told your true self is not real.

For many people, the pressure to fit into one of two sanctioned gender narratives is itself a form of chronic coercion. The system demands a simplified identity so it can assign you a predictable role. But human reality is more complex than institutional categories.

There are not only two genders.

Human expression is far more varied than the binary allows, and many people experience gender as fluid, plural, or evolving across time (Fausto-Sterling 2000). The violence is not in diversity; the violence is in forced conformity.

In a society that celebrates the mask, gender becomes one more arena where authenticity can be punished and performance rewarded.

This same logic applies to all the boxes bureaucratic forms require us to fit—race, ethnicity, nationality, disability status, class, even our looks—because once human complexity is forced into administrative categories, those categories can be used to rank, sort, discipline, and deny.

The End Goal: Matching Energy, Not Masks

If the mask is survival, then healing is the restoration of safety.

The end goal is not to "stop masking" in some moralistic way—because sometimes masking is still necessary under coercive conditions. The end goal is to build enough internal and relational safety that you can increasingly exist without the mask and still feel protected.

That is the simplest definition of healing:

the growing ability to be real without becoming unsafe.

And from that place, something changes in how relationships form.

Instead of searching for people who approve of the mask, you begin searching for people whose nervous systems can meet your nervous system—people who can hold your reality without trying to edit it. The goal becomes resonance rather than performance.

Not "Who will validate the role I'm playing?"
But "Who matches my energy—my honesty, my pace, my depth, my tenderness?"

Because the true self does not heal in isolation. It heals in accurate reflection.

When we find matches in energy—people who do not require our self-erasure—we begin to reverse the cultural inversion. We begin to recognize that starving is not beautiful, that numbness is not strength, that domination is not leadership, and that being human is not a flaw.

We begin to remember what the system tried to rename.

And that remembering is political.

References

Bordo, Susan. 1993. *Unbearable Weight: Feminism, Western Culture, and the Body*. Berkeley: University of California Press.

Bruch, Hilde. 1973. *Eating Disorders: Obesity, Anorexia Nervosa, and the Person Within*. New York: Basic Books.

Butler, Judith. 1990. *Gender Trouble: Feminism and the Subversion of Identity*. New York: Routledge.

Fairburn, Christopher G. 2008. *Cognitive Behavior Therapy and Eating Disorders*. New York: Guilford Press.

Fausto-Sterling, Anne. 2000. *Sexing the Body: Gender Politics and the Construction of Sexuality*. New York: Basic Books.

Herman, Judith L. 1992. *Trauma and Recovery*. New York: Basic Books.

van der Kolk, Bessel. 2014. *The Body Keeps the Score: Brain, Mind, and Body in the Healing of Trauma*. New York: Viking.

Wolf, Naomi. 1991. *The Beauty Myth: How Images of Beauty Are Used Against Women*. New York: William Morrow.

Chapter 6

Trauma Bond And Bystander Effect

A greed-addicted system does not survive on force alone. It survives through psychology—through the way fear reorganizes attachment and the way crowds outsource conscience. Two patterns are especially useful to such a system: **trauma bonding** and the **bystander effect**. Together they explain something people often struggle to name: why harm can become normal, why victims can remain attached to the very structures that injure them, and why witnesses so often do nothing—even when they privately know what is happening is wrong.

This chapter is not about blaming individuals for being trapped. It is about exposing the mechanisms that keep people trapped so the spell can break.

---

1) Trauma bonding: attachment under threat

Trauma bonding describes a bond that forms when care and harm are intertwined—especially under conditions of power imbalance, intermittent reinforcement, and fear. The person is not "choosing abuse." They are adapting to unpredictability. When cruelty is mixed with moments of relief, attention, or apparent kindness, the nervous system learns to cling to the small windows of safety as if they were the whole truth (Dutton and Painter 1981; Herman 1992).

Imagine a helpless child living with a toxic parent. It isn't that the child can't see the dysfunction and the hurt; it's that the power dynamic becomes normalized, and breaking free is not an option if the child wants to stay alive. In that situation, the child often has only one workable strategy: to construct a more tolerable version of the parent in their mind—a docile, reasonable, "maybe they didn't mean it" version—so that daily life doesn't feel impossible.

That strategy can protect the child physically, but it can injure the psyche. It turns mistreatment into something explainable, even justified, and the child may carry that internalized distortion into adulthood. Later, when similar dynamics appear in friendships, workplaces, or intimate relationships, the person may repeat the same adaptation—minimizing harm, rationalizing cruelty, and clinging to the hope that if they behave correctly, the other person will finally become the safer version they once had to imagine.

Intermittent reinforcement is one of the strongest conditioning schedules known: unpredictable rewards can produce compulsive persistence (Ferster and Skinner 1957). In relational life, this looks like the cycle many survivors recognize: rupture → terror → small repair → relief → renewed hope → deeper attachment—followed by the next rupture. The bond strengthens not because the relationship is healthy, but because the nervous system becomes organized around the relief of not being punished *this time*.

This is why trauma bonding can feel like love while functioning like captivity. It is attachment built on survival math.

---

2) The system-level version: institutions as trauma-bonding machines

Trauma bonding doesn't only happen between individuals. It can happen between people and institutions.

Institutions can harm people—through bureaucratic denial, dismissal, or extraction—and then offer tiny intermittent rewards: approval, access, a promotion, a small grant, a temporary benefit, a "we hear you" statement, a minimal accommodation, a token apology. The system injures and then provides just enough relief to keep the person engaged, hopeful, and compliant.

This is a political version of intermittent reinforcement.

For many people living with **CRC-PTSD**, the bond is not to one abuser but to a repeating pattern across settings: school, work, healthcare, family, bureaucracy—places you can't avoid yet, dignity is conditional and safety must be earned (Freyd 1996). Over time, the nervous system learns that connection is precarious and must be managed carefully. People become hyper-attuned to authority moods, vague rules, and social cues. They fawn, perform, self-edit, and over-function because the environment has trained them to treat stability as something granted by power.

In a greed-addicted society, this attachment-to-power becomes structurally useful: people remain psychologically invested in systems that wound them because leaving feels like loss of safety—even when staying is harmful.

---

3) The bystander effect: when conscience is outsourced

If trauma bonding explains why people remain attached to harmful systems, the bystander effect helps explain why harm becomes socially tolerated.

The bystander effect refers to the tendency for individuals to be less likely to help in an emergency when other people are present. Responsibility diffuses: "Someone else will act." Ambiguity increases: "Maybe it's not that serious." Social cues dominate: "No one else is reacting, so maybe it's normal" (Darley and Latané 1968; Latané and Darley 1970). Decades of research, including large meta-analyses, show the effect is real, though its size varies by context and perceived danger (Fischer et al. 2011).

In institutions, the bystander effect becomes a bureaucracy. Harm is routed through departments. Decisions are fragmented. Accountability is dispersed. Each person plays a small role that feels insufficient to matter—so no one feels responsible for the whole.

This is how a system can produce harm "without anyone doing it."

---

4) How these two patterns reinforce each other

Trauma bonding and the bystander effect form a closed loop:

- The victim learns that speaking up risks punishment or abandonment, so they adapt through performance and silence.
- The witness learns that speaking up risks social cost, career cost, or conflict, so they adapt through avoidance.
- The institution benefits from both forms of adaptation because the harm continues without overt coercion.

Over time, the system trains a population to treat ethical clarity as dangerous.

This is why people can privately acknowledge injustice and still participate. It is not always because they are cruel. It is often because they are afraid—and because the social environment rewards compliance and punishes disruption.

Bandura's concept of **moral disengagement** is useful here: people learn psychological maneuvers that allow them to participate in harm while preserving a self-image of goodness—euphemistic language, diffusion of responsibility, minimizing consequences, blaming the victim, "I was just doing my job" (Bandura 1999). Classic research on obedience and roles shows how quickly ordinary people can participate in harmful systems when authority and social structure support it (Milgram 1974; Zimbardo 2007). This is closely aligned with Hannah Arendt's notion of the **banality of evil**—the idea that profound harm is often carried out not by monstrous individuals, but by ordinary people performing routinized tasks within systems that normalize cruelty and convert conscience into procedure (Arendt 1963).

A greed-addicted system doesn't need everyone to be a villain. It only needs enough people to be numb, busy, and afraid.

---

5) What this does to the soul: CRC-PTSD as a social outcome

When a society routinely forces people into these roles—victim, bystander, reluctant participant—it produces collective dysregulation.

All the parties develop CRC-PTSD patterns: chronic threat vigilance, self-doubt, distrust, and the internalized belief that safety requires masking. Those witnessing harm without acting develop a subtler injury, and those required to carry out harmful policies to survive can become numb as a form of self-protection—because feeling the full moral reality of what they are doing would be psychologically intolerable.

This is one reason greed addiction escalates: numbness becomes professional, cruelty becomes normal, and the truth-teller becomes "the problem."

---

6) Breaking the loop: the Truth-Teller intervention

Trauma bonding breaks when the nervous system stops confusing intermittent relief with love. The bystander effect breaks when responsibility becomes personal again.

Truth-telling does both.

Truth-telling names:

- the pattern (intermittent harm + intermittent reward)
- the cost (what it does to bodies, communities, and meaning)
- the social dynamics (diffusion of responsibility, normalization, fear)

But truth-telling is not only speech. It is **repairing perception**.

Some practical antidotes we all can engage in are:

A. Reduce ambiguity

Bystanders freeze when they can't name what they're seeing. Learn to name it plainly: "This is harm. This is exploitation. This is coercion. This is an abuse of power."

B. Make responsibility explicit

In groups: assign roles, decide who speaks, decide what action will be taken. Diffusion collapses when responsibility is named.

C. Build micro-networks of courage

One person speaking alone is easy to punish. A small aligned group is harder to silence.

D. Replace intermittent reinforcement with consistent care

Trauma bonds dissolve when someone experiences stable, non-transactional support. Consistency is medicine.

E. Practice "repair over punishment"

People are more willing to intervene when cultures treat mistakes as repairable rather than exiling. That's how you build a pro-intervention norm.

F. Teach nervous systems to tolerate conflict

Most bystanders don't act because their bodies register conflict as danger. In that sense, regulation skills are civic skills. Yet it would be naïve—and often unethical—to treat regulation as emotional suppression in the face of real harm. Anger and grief are not problems to eliminate; they are signals that something is wrong, and in a healthy society they must be allowed to become visible.

Capitalism often privatizes emotion, pushing distress into the personal sphere while dismissing public concern through "tone" policing—treating the manner of expression as more important than the content of what is being revealed. The task, then, is not to become emotionally silent, but to express emotion in ways that do not reproduce harm: to channel anger and grief into clear language, collective action, and honest truth-telling rather than into cruelty or scapegoating.

---

7) The political meaning of intervention

In a greed-addicted society, the deepest control strategy is to keep people isolated, ashamed, and uncertain. Trauma bonding and bystander passivity are not merely psychological quirks; they become mechanisms of social order.

So the opposite is also true:

- Consistent care is political.
- Shared clarity is political.
- Collective intervention is political.
- Repairing moral perception is political.

When people stop outsourcing conscience and stop calling intermittent relief "love," the system loses its easiest fuel.

And that is how recovery begins.

References

Ainsworth, Mary D. S., Mary C. Blehar, Everett Waters, and Sally Wall. 1978. *Patterns of Attachment: A Psychological Study of the Strange Situation*. Hillsdale, NJ: Lawrence Erlbaum.

Arendt, Hannah. 1963. *Eichmann in Jerusalem: A Report on the Banality of Evil.* New York: Viking Press.

Bandura, Albert. 1999. "Moral Disengagement in the Perpetration of Inhumanities." *Personality and Social Psychology Review* 3(3):193–209.

Darley, John M., and Bibb Latané. 1968. "Bystander Intervention in Emergencies: Diffusion of Responsibility." *Journal of Personality and Social Psychology* 8(4):377–383.

Dutton, Donald G., and Susan L. Painter. 1981. "Traumatic Bonding: The Development of Emotional Attachments in Battered Women and Other Relationships of Intermittent Abuse." *Victimology* 6(1–4):139–155.

Ferster, C. B., and B. F. Skinner. 1957. *Schedules of Reinforcement.* New York: Appleton-Century-Crofts.

Fischer, Peter, Tobias Greitemeyer, Fabian Pollozek, and Dieter Frey. 2011. "The Bystander-Effect: A Meta-Analytic Review on Bystander Intervention in Dangerous and Non-Dangerous Emergencies." *Psychological Bulletin* 137(4):517–537.

Freyd, Jennifer J. 1996. *Betrayal Trauma: The Logic of Forgetting Childhood Abuse.* Cambridge, MA: Harvard University Press.

Herman, Judith L. 1992. *Trauma and Recovery.* New York: Basic Books.

Latané, Bibb, and John M. Darley. 1970. *The Unresponsive Bystander: Why Doesn't He Help?* New York: Appleton-Century-Crofts.

Milgram, Stanley. 1974. *Obedience to Authority: An Experimental View*. New York: Harper & Row.

Zimbardo, Philip. 2007. *The Lucifer Effect: Understanding How Good People Turn Evil.* New York: Random House.

Chapter 7

Addiction Escalation: Power

Power is often framed as competence. In public narratives, those who accumulate influence are described as decisive, visionary, and strong. But power can also function as an emotional substitute—especially in cultures where vulnerability is punished and connection is made conditional.

In the previous chapters, we traced how a fragile self can be armored through performance, how emotional numbing becomes a mask that looks like success, and how scarcity logic trains entire populations to compete for approval and safety. Here we reach the escalation point: the moment power is no longer merely an instrument to achieve goals, but becomes the primary strategy for regulating the self.

This is the addiction's evolution.

When connection is unsafe, power begins to look like the next best thing.

---

1. The Psychological Angle: Control as a Substitute for Belonging

Human beings are wired for co-regulation. We do not learn safety alone; we learn it through relationships. When relationships are consistently available, the nervous system internalizes stability and the self can soften. But when relationships are unreliable, humiliating, or conditional, the nervous system adapts by seeking insulation.

Power offers insulation.

It reduces dependence on others. It minimizes exposure to rejection. It creates distance from vulnerability. And because it can produce immediate relief, it becomes reinforcing. Not unlike other addictions, the cycle begins with a simple learning process: **this reduces discomfort, do it again**.

Over time, a subtle shift occurs. The person is no longer seeking power to accomplish something meaningful; they are seeking power to avoid something terrifying—exposure, dependence, and the risk of being seen without the mask.

This is where connection is replaced by domination.

It is not always conscious. It can present as "standards," "leadership," "excellence," "efficiency," "being realistic." But the underlying function is often the same: reducing relational uncertainty through hierarchy. If people are beneath you, they cannot abandon you in the same way. If you control resources, you do not have to ask for care. If you can purchase compliance, you do not have to risk intimacy.

Power becomes the defense against relational pain.

---

2. The Attachment Angle: Avoiding the Cost of Dependence

Attachment theory helps clarify why power can become especially seductive (Bowlby 1969). When early attachment experiences teach a person that needing others is dangerous, they may develop strategies of emotional self-sufficiency. In adulthood, these strategies can look like competence and independence. But at the extremes, they can become an avoidance of intimacy.

Power is the perfect tool for avoidance because it offers a controlled form of relationship.

A hierarchy is a relationship without mutuality. It is interaction without the risk of equal vulnerability. It is connection with an exit hatch: if the relationship becomes uncomfortable, you can fire someone, replace them, withdraw resources, or retreat into status.

This is one reason greed addiction and relational disconnection so often travel together. If someone cannot risk being truly known, they may pursue forms of "connection" that do not require exposure. Influence, reputation, and admiration can mimic relational warmth while keeping the self protected.

But admiration is not attachment.

It does not mirror the real self back.

It mirrors the mask.

---

3. The Neurobiological Angle: Escalation, Tolerance, and the Plateau

Addictions escalate because the nervous system adapts. What once produced a strong emotional effect becomes baseline. The person must intensify the stimulus to recreate the same relief or activation (Koob and Le Moal 2001).

Power follows this pattern.

At first, a promotion, a raise, or public recognition produces a rush. The nervous system feels expanded—safer, larger, less vulnerable. But the effect fades. The person acclimates. The baseline shifts.

Then more is needed.

More money. More control. More reach. More dominance. More exemption from rules.

And because power is relational—because it is experienced through comparison—there is no natural endpoint. Someone always has more. Someone always threatens your position. The environment of hierarchy keeps the nervous system in a state of vigilance.

This is the escalation trap: the very strategy used to reduce insecurity eventually reproduces it.

---

4. The Moral Angle: Empathy Becomes a Threat

As power replaces connection, empathy begins to feel dangerous.

Empathy is a form of relational permeability. It allows another person's reality to enter your nervous system. It challenges self-justification. It creates moral friction or cognitive dissonance.

But exploitation requires smooth functioning.

Systems of extraction do not run well when decision-makers remain emotionally open to the suffering they produce. As a result, many power structures reward emotional detachment. Compassion is reframed as weakness. Sensitivity is reframed as instability. The "truth-teller" becomes the problem—not because they are wrong, but because they interrupt the psychological economy of the system.

This is how the addiction protects itself.

It labels empathy as weakness.

It treats conscience as interference.

---

5. The Economic Angle: When Growth Becomes a Withdrawal Avoidance

At a systemic level, the escalation of greed is not merely psychological—it is built into economic design.

Modern economies often treat growth as a necessity rather than a choice. Corporations are evaluated by quarterly expansion. Markets punish stagnation. Investors demand increasing returns. A company that says "we have enough" appears irrational within a growth-obsessed framework.

This creates a **structural** equivalence to **addiction**:

- expansion functions like a dose
- stagnation feels like withdrawal
- limits feel like threat

- redistribution feels like loss
- sufficiency feels like death

In this sense, the system behaves like an addict: **it must keep expanding in order to avoid collapse.** And because growth eventually encounters real limits—ecological, social, psychological—the system compensates by **intensifying extraction**: lower wages, higher rents, monetizing attention, privatizing public goods, turning healthcare and education into markets, and transforming human life into data and commodity.

Power replaces connection not only in individuals but in institutions. Markets become the medium through which people relate. Human needs become "**demand**." Relationships become "**networking**." Care becomes "**service provision.**" The economy reorganizes social life into transactions.

The result is a society that grows richer in wealth while becoming poorer in relational trust, humanity and meaning .

---

6. The Cultural Angle: The Empire of Comparison

The addiction escalates culturally through comparison.

In a world saturated with images of wealth and curated success, people internalize the idea that their worth must be proven. This produces mass masking and mass insecurity. Individuals begin to compete not only for resources but for legitimacy—trying to appear successful enough to be treated with dignity.

This is how greed becomes contagious.

Even those harmed by the system may be drawn to its symbols because symbols of success promise relief from humiliation. The system does not only exploit people materially; **it colonizes desire.**

It teaches the population to want what hurts them.

---

7. Long-Term Effects: What Happens If This Continues?

If greed addiction continues to escalate, the long-term outcomes are not subtle. They are structural.

Relational collapse.
As power replaces connection, trust erodes. Communities weaken. People retreat into isolation and survival logic. Cooperation becomes harder because everyone expects exploitation. Social life becomes more transactional.

Institutional hardening.
Institutions become more punitive and less human. Bureaucracies become more automated. Decisions are made by metrics rather than relationships. Those who do not "perform" become disposable.

Psychological flattening.
Nervous systems adapt to chronic insecurity through numbing, dissociation, and hypervigilance. CRC-PTSD becomes normalized across populations. People lose access to meaning and begin to treat exhaustion as normal adulthood.

Political fragmentation.
Scarcity narratives intensify division. Groups are pitted against each other for shrinking resources while wealth concentrates upward. Rather than challenging power, people fight laterally.

Ecological breach.
A growth-addicted system collides with planetary limits. When the ideology of "more" encounters ecological reality, elites often respond by intensifying extraction and securing private protection rather than restructuring the system.

A new caste of insulation.
The wealthy increasingly purchase distance from social breakdown: private healthcare, private security, private education, gated communities, and disaster preparedness. This deepens moral disconnection. The less one shares conditions with others, the easier it is to justify abandonment.

This is the endpoint of power replacing connection: a society where the privileged live behind walls—physical and psychological—and the rest are forced into survival competition.

At that point, greed is no longer a personal vice.

It becomes a civilizational pathology. It leads to the fall of an Empire, in which masses die and suffer from scarcity, bureaucracy, fear, and overwork.

---

8. The Intervention: Rebuilding Connection as a Form of Recovery

In addiction treatment, recovery is not simply about stopping the substance. It is about rebuilding the conditions that made the substance necessary.

The same is true here.

If power has replaced connection, then recovery must involve restoring the capacity for connection—both individually and structurally. The end goal is not moral perfection; it is the ability to feel safe without domination, safe without the mask, safe without constant escalation.

This requires:

- Relational environments where authenticity is not punished. People who can tolerate and co-regulate anger, fear and loss together. Healing and grieving circles.

- Institutions that protect dignity without requiring performance. No fake poverty line and arbitrary eligibility theater.

- Economic structures that reward sufficiency rather than endless growth. Normalization of enough.

- Cultural narratives that define success as aliveness, authentic connections, care, and not accumulation.

The addiction escalates when people cannot find safety in relationships.

The healing begins when people can.

References

Bowlby, John. 1969. *Attachment and Loss: Volume 1. Attachment.* New York: Basic Books.

Koob, George F., and Michel Le Moal. 2001. "Drug Addiction, Dysregulation of Reward, and Allostasis." *Neuropsychopharmacology* 24(2):97–129.

Piketty, Thomas. 2014. *Capital in the Twenty-First Century.* Cambridge, MA: Harvard University Press.

Polanyi, Karl. 1944. *The Great Transformation.* Boston: Beacon Press.

PART III

How We Celebrate An Illness

CHAPTER 8

Greed Produced Scarcity

Scarcity is often presented as a natural condition of human life. We are told that resources are limited, that competition is inevitable, and that societies must organize themselves around difficult trade-offs. Within this narrative, inequality appears almost unavoidable. Some people succeed because they work harder, innovate more effectively, or make better decisions. Others fall behind.

But this story collapses under closer examination.

Modern societies do not operate under conditions of true scarcity. The world currently produces more than enough food to feed every human being, yet hunger persists in many regions. Oil is no longer the only source of energy. We have access to clean energy. Global economic productivity has reached levels unimaginable in previous centuries, yet millions of people struggle to secure stable housing, healthcare, or basic economic security (Piketty 2014; Sen 1999). Universities increasingly train scientists not to expand knowledge, but to commercialize it—through products, patents, and subscription-based access to tools that should be basic public goods.

The problem, therefore, is not scarcity itself.

The problem is **distribution**.

Scarcity, in many cases, is not a natural condition but a **constructed one**.

The Historical Roots of Manufactured Scarcity

For much of human history, many communities organized resources through forms of shared access, reciprocal obligation, and collective use of land. While inequality and hierarchy certainly existed, the scale of accumulation characteristic of modern economic systems was relatively uncommon (Graeber and Wengrow 2021).

One major transformation occurred with the enclosure of common lands in early modern Europe. Through legal reforms such as the **Enclosure Acts**, lands that had historically supported shared subsistence practices were gradually privatized and transferred into the control of landowners (Polanyi 1944).

Communities that once relied on these lands for survival were displaced and forced into wage labor.

Scarcity was not simply discovered.

It was **produced through legal and economic restructuring**.

Colonial expansion intensified these processes. European imperial powers extracted vast quantities of resources from colonized territories while reorganizing local economies to serve distant markets. Land, labor, and agricultural production were redirected toward imperial wealth accumulation (Rodney 1972).

These processes generated enormous wealth at imperial centers while producing instability and deprivation across colonized regions.

Scarcity was not an accidental outcome.
It was embedded in the design of the system.

And over time, that design evolved. Early colonial projects often required visible borders—ships, armies, treaties, plantations, and explicit domination of land and bodies. But as capitalism matured, extraction learned to become less geographically obvious. Colonization increasingly shifted from territorial occupation to **structural dependence**: debt, trade rules, intellectual property regimes, and institutional "development" frameworks that kept resources flowing upward without the same need for direct rule.

Eventually, colonization stopped requiring borders.

In the digital age, a new layer intensified this process: **psychological operations** and attention capitalism. Social media did not simply connect people; it reorganized perception. It trained populations to internalize elite ideologies of worth—wealth as intelligence, productivity as virtue, visibility as legitimacy. Algorithmic systems amplified what was already rewarded: status signaling, competition, outrage, and comparison. As a result, the scarcity narrative moved inside people. Individuals began measuring their lives through curated images, follower counts, prestige cues, and performative "success," often without recognizing that these were not neutral measures but cultural scripts optimized for profit.

Social media then became an echo chamber not merely of opinions, but of **hierarchies**. It circulated the same competitive myths—merit, hustle, branding, self-optimization—until they felt like common sense. In that environment, people could be living through real material precarity while still being psychologically recruited into admiration of the very system that produced it.

Scarcity became both economic and epistemic: a shortage of resources, and a shortage of truthful ways to interpret reality.

Law as Pseudo-Science, Patents as Knowledge Control, and the Gaslighting of Inner Knowing

One of the most consequential shifts in modernity is that **law began to present itself as a kind of neutral science**—a technical system of rules, classifications, and "objective" procedures. Like religion once did, law developed a specialized language that claims legitimacy by sounding impersonal, universal, and rational. But this language often functions less to discover truth than to **stabilize power**. When a society treats legal language as inherently superior to lived experience, it becomes possible to translate harm into technicalities: *jurisdiction, standing, liability, compliance, due process*. The lived reality remains, but it is reframed as "inadmissible," "unproven," "not actionable," or simply "not within scope." In this way, law becomes a kind of secular priesthood—granting moral permission through procedure, and laundering violence into legitimacy (Weber 1978; Foucault 1977).

This "scientization" of authority does not stop at law. It spreads into how knowledge itself is regulated. **Patenting became a central mechanism for controlling what should be shared**—not by selling "knowing" directly (because knowing cannot be owned in any deep human sense), but by enclosing the practical applications of knowledge behind property rights. The result is a paradox: knowledge is said to be universal, but its use is privatized. The commons of human understanding is converted into monopoly control over methods, tools, and access—especially in technology, pharmaceuticals, and agriculture. This is why the patent system often functions less as a reward for creativity than as a gatekeeping device that determines who may build, who may heal, and who may participate in the future (Drahos and Braithwaite 2002; Boyle 2003).

At the same time, modernity created an **epistemic hierarchy**—a ranked system of "legitimate knowledge"—and then trained people to internalize it. The scientific method is invaluable for many purposes, but the *cultural* story built around it often became a tool of control: only certain questions count, only certain kinds of evidence count, only certain forms of language count, only certain institutions can certify reality. This is how power protects itself through "the illusion of objectivity": by defining what counts as truth in advance, and then dismissing other forms of knowing—embodied experience, moral intuition, communal memory, trauma knowledge, relational truth—as "subjective." The result is not science as inquiry, but scientism as gatekeeping: a mechanism that narrows legitimacy and distributes credibility upward (Bourdieu 1984; Santos 2014; Jasanoff 2004).

Finally, marketing and psychological operations intensified this structure into something more intimate: **the systematic erosion of self-trust**. Once institutions control legitimacy, the next step is controlling perception. People can be trained to doubt their own reality, their own bodily truth, and even their own moral instincts—especially when those instincts conflict with the system's profit needs. This is how epistemic control becomes psychological control: you no longer have to silence people directly if you can convince them they are unreliable witnesses to their own lives. "Your feelings are irrational." "Your perception is biased." "Your suffering is just your mindset." "Your outrage is the problem—fix your tone." This is institutional gaslighting at scale: not merely the denial of facts, but the re-engineering of what people are allowed to treat as real. And once people stop trusting their internal sense of good and bad, they become governable through metrics, authority, and branding—precisely the conditions a greed-addicted system requires (Foucault 1977; Herman 1992; Mirowski 2013).

This is the deeper architecture of control: law creates the language of legitimacy; patents enclose the commons of knowledge; epistemic hierarchy determines whose reality counts; and marketing trains the public to mistrust their own perception. The end result is not merely inequality of wealth—it is **inequality of *reality*.** Recovery, then, is not only economic. It is epistemic and moral: rebuilding the capacity to trust the body's truth, to recognize harm even when it is legalized, and to reclaim knowing as a human commons rather than a privately owned permission structure.

Scarcity as an Ideology

Over time, scarcity evolved from an economic condition into an **ideological framework**.

Economic thought increasingly framed competition as the primary mechanism through which resources should be distributed. The assumption that there is never enough—jobs, opportunity, security—became normalized and moralized.

This narrative performs an important function.

If scarcity is natural, inequality appears inevitable and natural too.

If scarcity is natural, those who accumulate extraordinary wealth appear to have simply succeeded in a difficult competition.

The structure of the system itself disappears from view. Differences in wealth and opportunity are instead explained through individual outcomes or through categories such as race, gender, and nationality, obscuring how these divisions have historically been used to organize labor, distribute resources, and maintain unequal systems of power.

This dynamic closely mirrors what I describe in *The Truth Teller: Transforming Our World* as **institutional gaslighting**. When systemic structures produce widespread insecurity, individuals are encouraged to interpret their struggles as personal failures rather than structural conditions.

The system produces the wound and then diffuses responsibility by gaslighting us to believe it's a personal failure.

The Language of Scarcity

Language plays a critical role in maintaining this illusion.

Modern economic discourse is saturated with metaphors of limitation and competition. Terms such as *human capital, labor markets*, and *competitive advantage* subtly frame human beings as economic units rather than participants in social relationships (Fourcade and Healy 2007).

Even the language of success reflects scarcity thinking. People are described as “getting ahead,” “falling behind,” or “winning the race.”

But a race implies a fixed number of winners.

When language frames life as competition, cooperation begins to appear unrealistic or naïve.

Language does not simply describe reality; it shapes the way reality is perceived (Lakoff and Johnson 1980).

Over time, scarcity becomes internalized. Individuals begin to interpret their lives through the same competitive lens embedded in economic language.

Someone will always have more wealth, more recognition, or more security.

Under these conditions, the feeling of **never enough** becomes inevitable while the **internal void for connection** gets bigger.

Scarcity and the Commodification of the Self

Once scarcity becomes internalized, it becomes economically profitable.

Entire industries have emerged to help individuals cope with the anxiety produced by competitive environments. Self-improvement markets promise to optimize productivity, enhance attractiveness, increase social influence, and accelerate career success.

These industries offer tools for navigating the system.

But they rarely question the system itself.

Instead, individuals are encouraged to continuously refine themselves—improving their bodies, skills, credentials, and personal brands. Sociologists have described this dynamic as the **marketization of the self**, in which individuals increasingly treat their identities as forms of economic capital (Brown 2015).

The person becomes both the consumer and the product.

But a product must always compete with other products.

And in a globalized world, there will always be someone better.

Scarcity therefore persists even in conditions of abundance.

The Political Function of Scarcity

Scarcity is not only an economic condition or psychological experience.

It is also a political tool.

When individuals believe resources are limited, they are more likely to compete with one another rather than challenge the systems that organize distribution. Energy that might otherwise be directed toward collective action becomes absorbed in personal survival.

This fragmentation benefits systems of concentrated power.

Individuals struggling to secure their own stability have little capacity to question the broader architecture of inequality.

Scarcity therefore functions as a mechanism of social control.

People remain busy competing.

The system remains unquestioned.

References

Boyle, James. 2003. "The Second Enclosure Movement and the Construction of the Public Domain." *Law and Contemporary Problems* 66(1/2):33–74.

Bourdieu, Pierre. 1984. *Distinction: A Social Critique of the Judgement of Taste*. Cambridge, MA: Harvard University Press.

Brown, Wendy. 2015. *Undoing the Demos: Neoliberalism's Stealth Revolution*. New York: Zone Books.

Drahos, Peter, and John Braithwaite. 2002. *Information Feudalism: Who Owns the Knowledge Economy?* New York: The New Press.

Foucault, Michel. 1977. *Discipline and Punish: The Birth of the Prison*. New York: Pantheon.

Fourcade, Marion, and Kieran Healy. 2007. "Moral Views of Market Society." *Annual Review of Sociology* 33:285–311.

Graeber, David, and David Wengrow. 2021. *The Dawn of Everything: A New History of Humanity*. New York: Farrar, Straus and Giroux.

Herman, Judith L. 1992. *Trauma and Recovery*. New York: Basic Books.

Jasanoff, Sheila, ed. 2004. *States of Knowledge: The Co-Production of Science and Social Order*. London: Routledge.

Lakoff, George, and Mark Johnson. 1980. *Metaphors We Live By*. Chicago: University of Chicago Press.

Mirowski, Philip. 2013. *Never Let a Serious Crisis Go to Waste: How Neoliberalism Survived the Financial Meltdown*. London: Verso.

Piketty, Thomas. 2014. *Capital in the Twenty-First Century*. Cambridge, MA: Harvard University Press.

Polanyi, Karl. 1944. *The Great Transformation: The Political and Economic Origins of Our Time*. Boston: Beacon Press.

Rodney, Walter. 1972. *How Europe Underdeveloped Africa*. London: Bogle-L'Ouverture.

Santos, Boaventura de Sousa. 2014. *Epistemologies of the South: Justice Against Epistemicide*. Boulder, CO: Paradigm Publishers.

Sen, Amartya. 1999. *Development as Freedom*. Oxford: Oxford University Press.

Weber, Max. 1978. *Economy and Society: An Outline of Interpretive Sociology*. Edited by Guenther Roth and Claus Wittich. Berkeley: University of California Press.

Wilkinson, Richard, and Kate Pickett. 2009. *The Spirit Level: Why Greater Equality Makes Societies Stronger*. New York: Bloomsbury Press.

Chapter 9

The Myth of Personal Responsibility

The phrase *personal responsibility* sounds reasonable. It signals adulthood, agency, accountability. It appeals to a basic moral instinct: that our choices matter, and that people should not be absolved of harm they cause.

But in modern economic life, *personal responsibility* has become something else.

It has become a story powerful enough to conceal the structure of the world.

Not because responsibility is irrelevant, but because the phrase is routinely used to divert attention from the material reality that shapes choice—resources, institutions, and unequal starting conditions. It converts structural design into personal deficiency and recasts a rigged environment as a fair test. In doing so, it often treats morality, trust, and empathy as weaknesses, as if judgments about merit and deservingness could be made from some neutral vantage point.

But there is no view from nowhere. There are only views from people—positioned in histories, interests, and power relations. And the "objective" standards we are told to live by—rules, laws, credentials, and merit measures—are not natural laws. They are human constructions that reflect particular values and serve particular arrangements of power.

Humans also crave order because order can feel like safety. We cling to patterns even when the pattern is harmful. In abusive relationships, predictability can feel more bearable than uncertainty—not because the abuse is acceptable, but because the nervous system learns, *at least I know what to expect; at least I've survived this before.* That same impulse toward certainty shows up socially: we simplify human complexity into binaries, rankings, and neat categories, even though those simplifications can never capture the full reality of a human life.

This is how the story becomes so seductive:

If a person is thriving, the story says they earned it.
If a person is struggling, the story says they failed.

It is clean.

It is simple.

And it is often false—not because choices do not matter, but because choices are not made in equal conditions, and the "rules" of the game were written by human hands, not by nature.

Life Is Not a Single Moment — It's a compounding Timeline

One reason the myth persists is that people evaluate life as though it were a snapshot: an individual at a single moment, making a single decision. But life is not a snapshot. It is a timeline. And the timeline compounds.

Resources compound.
Deprivation compounds.

Support compounds.
Stress compounds.
Health compounds.
Connections compound.
Time compounds.
Beauty compounds
Poverty compounds.

Small early advantages can widen into enormous differences over years because they reduce friction at every stage. Small early losses can do the same, because they add friction at every stage.

This is what the myth of personal responsibility cannot admit, because it relies on a fantasy: that everyone begins the race at roughly the same starting line, and that the outcome reflects effort alone.

But reality is closer to this:

Some people begin with safety. Others begin with chaos.
Some people begin with a cushion. Others begin with debt.
Some people begin with a body that is cared for. Others begin with untreated trauma.
Some people begin with a network. Others begin with isolation.

And these differences do not disappear over time. They multiply.

Human-Made Merit Units

The myth also depends on a second assumption: that the units used to measure "merit" are neutral.

Grades.
Degrees.
Job titles.
Credit scores.
Gaps in a résumé.
Productivity metrics.
"Professionalism."
Even body standards.

These are not laws of nature. They are human-made measurements that reward some forms of life and punish others. They are treated as objective indicators of worth, even when they function as sorting mechanisms for access to resources.

A person does not fail because they lacked merit.

Often, they fail because they were filtered out by the system's chosen metrics.

And those metrics were designed within particular histories: histories of class hierarchy, racial hierarchy, gender hierarchy, ableism, and national inequality. The system's measurements are not simply measuring ability—they are measuring conformity to what the system already recognizes.

So "personal responsibility" becomes a kind of moral theater: the system creates the rules, then blames individuals for failing to win at the game.

An Addict: "Bad Choices" or a Rigged Nervous System?

Consider the addict.

The moral narrative says: they chose it. They should have more discipline. They should simply stop. Their suffering becomes proof of personal failure.

But addiction is rarely explained by a single choice. It is more often explained by accumulation—of trauma, stress, isolation, and the absence of stable support. Many people reach substances or compulsive behaviors not because they want destruction, but because they are trying to regulate pain in the only way that has worked quickly enough to keep them alive.

Now add the resource layer.

If the addict is wealthy, their addiction is treated as a "struggle" and they are offered rehabilitation, privacy, and second chances. If the addict is poor, their addiction is treated as a crime or a moral flaw and they are offered punishment, surveillance, and shame. They most likely lose their job and home.

The same condition yields radically different life outcomes depending on class and institutional response.

So is it personal responsibility?

Or is it a system that offers care to some and punishment to others—then calls the outcomes "deserved"?

A Homeless Person: The "Bad Decision" Myth

Consider a homeless person.

The myth says: they didn't work hard enough. They made poor choices. They must have done something wrong.

But homelessness is often a convergence point, not a starting point. It can follow:

- job loss
- untreated illness
- disability
- domestic violence
- rising rent
- family rejection
- bureaucratic denial of support
- the simple fact that housing has been transformed into an investment asset rather than shelter

If housing costs rise faster than wages, if healthcare costs can bankrupt the employed, if safety nets require extreme proof of suffering, then homelessness is not a personal anomaly. It is a predictable outcome for some portion of the population.

The myth keeps this invisible.

It turns a structural failure into a personal character judgment.

The Full-Time Worker: Working and Still Falling Behind

Now consider the full-time worker.

In the myth, full-time work is supposed to provide stability. "Get a job" becomes the moral solution to almost everything.

But in many modern economies, full-time work does not guarantee survival. Wages stagnate while the cost of housing, healthcare, education, and food rises. People can work continuously and still live one emergency away from collapse.

Yet the narrative persists: if you are struggling, you must not be trying hard enough.

This is not only economically inaccurate—it is psychologically violent.

It trains people to interpret systemic instability as personal inadequacy. It produces shame rather than clarity.

The Double-Job Worker: Discipline Becomes a Trap

Consider the person working two jobs.

This person is often praised as responsible. Disciplined. Hardworking. Inspirational.

But what does it mean that survival requires two jobs?

What does it mean that "responsibility" is defined as sacrificing sleep, health, relationships, and sanity to meet basic needs?

This is where the myth becomes cruel: it frames exploitation as virtue. It applauds self-erasure and calls it character.

A person may work two jobs and still be one car repair away from disaster. They may miss time with children, lose health, and never rest. Their body becomes the sacrifice that keeps the system functioning.

And the system calls it admirable.

Poor and Rich: The Same Action, Different Moral Meaning

Now consider the difference between poor and rich.

If a poor person misses a payment, they are "irresponsible."
If a rich person avoids taxes, they are "smart."

If a poor person receives assistance, they are "dependent."
If a rich person receives subsidies, they are "incentivized."

If a poor person cannot access healthcare, that is "unfortunate."
If a rich person cannot access luxury care, that is "outrage."

Even the language shifts. The moral story is tailored to protect power.

And that is the point: personal responsibility becomes a selective moral lens. It is applied downward, not upward. It disciplines the vulnerable while excusing the powerful.

The Deep Function of the Myth

The myth of personal responsibility does something politically precise.

It prevents collective recognition. It is the double standard manipulation tactic that gaslights us to see good as bad and bad as good.

If people believe their pain is personal, they will compete rather than unite. They will blame themselves rather than question the system. They will buy self-improvement products instead of demanding structural change.

This is why the myth pairs so well with greed addiction. A greed-addicted system requires a population that internalizes failure. It requires people to experience structural harm as private shame.

When this happens, people become governable through insecurity.

They become the perfect consumers: always striving, always optimizing, never arriving.

The Truth That Breaks the Spell

A more accurate question than “Who is responsible?” is often:

Could fair access to resources have changed the outcome?

If the answer is yes, then the problem is not merely individual choices.

It is the structure of opportunity.

That does not eliminate personal agency. It locates agency inside reality.

Personal responsibility matters most when people actually have choices.

The more a system removes real choices through scarcity, debt, unstable housing, and conditional care, the more "personal responsibility" becomes a cover story for structural violence.

What This Chapter Is Asking You to See

This chapter is not arguing that individuals are powerless.

It is arguing that the story of personal responsibility has been weaponized to protect inequality and cruelty.

It has trained us to see outcomes as moral proof instead of as evidence of resource distribution.

And once people accept that story, they begin to police themselves and one another—enforcing the system's cruelty while believing they are enforcing fairness.

That is how the myth reproduces itself.

Not through logic.

Through shame.

References

Bourdieu, Pierre. 1986. "The Forms of Capital." In *Handbook of Theory and Research for the Sociology of Education*, edited by J. G. Richardson, 241–258. New York: Greenwood.

Herman, Judith L. 1992. *Trauma and Recovery*. New York: Basic Books.

Mullainathan, Sendhil, and Eldar Shafir. 2013. *Scarcity: Why Having Too Little Means So Much*. New York: Times Books.

Sandel, Michael J. 2020. *The Tyranny of Merit: What's Become of the Common Good?* New York: Farrar, Straus and Giroux.

Chapter 10

Greed as a Systemic Addiction

It is tempting to treat greed as an individual flaw—an unfortunate personality trait expressed by a minority of especially selfish people. But the scale and consistency of modern extraction suggest something larger: greed has become institutionalized. It has been built into the operating logic of the economy, the design of organizations, and the cultural definitions of success. In that sense, greed is no longer merely a behavior. It is a system.

And systems can become addicted too.

Not metaphorically, but structurally: organized around escalation, unable to tolerate sufficiency, and destabilized by limits.

---

1. When "More" Becomes Non-Negotiable

Addiction is not only about desire; it is about the inability to stop despite harm. It is compulsive continuation even when the costs become obvious. The most recognizable marker of addiction is escalation: the need for increasing "doses" to maintain the same effect (Koob and Le Moal 2001). In a systemic context, the "dose" is growth. First farming, then oil, and now AI, perhaps space colonization next.

Modern economies are built around the assumption that growth must continue: profits must rise, markets must expand, productivity must increase, consumption must accelerate. An institution that announces "enough" is treated as irrational. A corporation that stabilizes rather than expands is punished by investors. A government that prioritizes sufficiency over expansion risks political backlash in a culture trained to equate growth with wellbeing.

This is the first signature of systemic addiction: **stagnation is experienced as threat.**

---

2. Corruption as a Design Feature, Not an Exception

When people say "the system is corrupt," the word *corrupt* is often used as a moral diagnosis: bad people in high places. But corruption is also structural. It emerges when institutional incentives consistently reward behaviors that harm the collective.

Once growth becomes the central requirement, the system begins to tolerate—then reward—actions that would otherwise be morally unacceptable. The logic is simple: if growth is sacred, then anything that increases growth becomes justified.

This is how exploitation becomes "efficiency."
How layoffs become "shareholder value."
How turning housing into an investment becomes "smart economics."
How privatizing care becomes "market innovation."

Karl Polanyi described this historical shift as a fundamental transformation: markets cease to be embedded within social life and instead social life becomes reorganized around markets

(Polanyi 1944). When market logic dominates, human needs are reclassified as "demand," and dignity becomes conditional on purchasing power.

In such a system, corruption is not occasional. It is functional.

---

3. How the System Trains the Human Nervous System

The system's most powerful achievement is not only economic. It is psychological.

It trains people to experience insecurity as normal and to treat optimization as the solution. It teaches individuals to interpret their worth through metrics: money, credentials, productivity, attractiveness, status. These metrics are presented as natural indicators of value, even though they are culturally constructed and historically tied to power (Bourdieu 1986; Brown 2015).

The result is a population that internalizes the system's demands.

People begin to manage themselves like companies: maximizing output, minimizing weakness, branding the self, making the self legible to institutional standards. When they feel pain, the system offers individual solutions—self-improvement, resilience training, productivity hacks—rather than structural change. This is not accidental. It keeps the system stable. It converts collective harm into private shame.

A greed-addicted system requires a particular kind of citizen: one who blames themselves, competes laterally, and keeps producing even when exhausted.

---

4. The Feedback Loop That Makes Greed Systemic

Once systemic addiction is in place, it reproduces itself through feedback loops:

- **Inequality fuels insecurity.**
  As wealth concentrates, more people experience precarity. Research on inequality shows that high-inequality societies tend to have lower social trust and worse health outcomes (Wilkinson and Pickett 2009).

- **Insecurity fuels compliance.**
  People with unstable housing, unstable healthcare, and unstable income have less capacity to resist or refuse exploitation. Survival becomes the full-time job.

- **Compliance fuels extraction.**
  Institutions extract more because they can. The system "learns" that it can push further without consequence.

- **Extraction increases inequality.**
  And the cycle intensifies.

This is systemic addiction: a self-reinforcing pattern that escalates harm while calling it normal.

---

5. The Long-Term Future of a Greed-Addicted System

If greed addiction continues unchecked, the long-term effects are predictable, not speculative.

1. **Permanent precarity for the majority.**
   As costs rise and protections shrink, more people will live in chronic instability. This is not only an economic condition; it is a psychological condition. It produces population-level dysregulation.

2. **Institutional hardening.**
   When inequality grows, institutions tend to become more punitive and more bureaucratic. Care becomes conditional. Access requires proof of suffering. The system builds filters rather than supports.

3. **Cultural narrowing.**
   Creativity, softness, and relational life become less accessible. People become more transactional. Friendship becomes networking. Community becomes brand alignment. Life becomes a résumé.

4. **Ecological collision.**
   Growth addiction collides with planetary limits. When the system cannot expand through new markets, it expands through intensified extraction—of land, bodies, attention, and time.

5. **A caste of insulation.**
   The wealthy increasingly buy distance from shared reality: private services, private security, private refuge. The less

the powerful share conditions with the rest, the easier abandonment becomes.

This is not a dystopian fantasy. It is the logical endpoint of a system that treats "more" as sacred and "enough" as failure. This is what leads to the fall of an empire.

---

6. The Solution: How Humans Free Themselves

A system-level addiction cannot be solved by asking individuals to become more ethical while leaving incentives intact. The system will continue to reward greed. And people under scarcity will continue to chase what looks like safety.

Freedom requires changing three layers at once: **psychological, cultural, and structural.**

A. Psychological liberation: withdrawing worth from the marketplace

The first act of freedom is refusing the system's measurement of human value. Not in a performative way, but in a nervous-system way: reclaiming the idea that worth is not something you earn through productivity, thinness, prestige, or profit.

This is not abstract. It is daily practice:

- building the capacity to feel safe without the mask
- recognizing that compulsive striving is often fear in disguise

- learning to locate "enough" internally rather than through comparison

This is how individuals stop being perfect consumers—always upgrading, always insufficient.

B. Cultural liberation: changing what we praise

A system survives because of what it celebrates.

If we want to end greed addiction, we have to stop calling:

- extraction "success"
- domination "leadership"
- burnout "ambition"
- starvation "discipline"
- moral numbness "strength"

We must reassign admiration to what sustains life:

- care work
- community-building
- truth-telling
- repair

- sufficiency

What a society praises is what it produces.

C. Structural liberation: building sufficiency into the rules

If the system is addicted, the rules must change so that "enough" becomes viable.

Examples of structural shifts that reduce systemic addiction:

- **decommodifying basics**: housing, healthcare, education, food security
- **limiting extraction**: stronger labor protections, anti-monopoly enforcement
- **redistributing power**: progressive taxation, inheritance limits, public investment
- **reducing coercion**: universal basic services so survival is not conditional on compliance
- **rebuilding common goods**: spaces and institutions where people are humans, not customers

The point is not a utopia. The point is lowering the baseline threat so people can stop living as if life is a competition for oxygen.

D. Relational liberation: returning to human-scale belonging

The system thrives when people are isolated. Connection creates resistance because it restores reality. When people are witnessed, they stop accepting gaslighting. When people are held, they stop mistaking domination for safety.

Human freedom is relational. The end goal is not independence from everyone. It is interdependence without coercion.

---

7. The Truth-Teller as the First Antidote

Addiction survives through denial.

Greed as a systemic addiction survives through a cultural agreement to call harm normal.

Truth-telling interrupts that agreement.

It says: this is not neutral.
It says: this is not natural.
It says: this is not inevitable.
It says: the numbers do not matter more than the lives.

The truth-teller does not merely criticize. The truth-teller restores moral perception. They bring the human back into view.

That is why systems punish truth-tellers.

Not because truth-tellers are wrong, but because truth threatens the mechanism that keeps the addiction running.

We need to intervene collectively, the way we would with any other addiction. It is difficult to go against the narratives we've been conditioned to believe about success and self-worth, but the shift can begin with a single reframe: seeing greed as a coping strategy rather than a virtue. Instead of shrinking in fear when we face power and greed, we can name what we are seeing, hold our ground, and respond with compassion for those suffering—without excusing harm and without surrendering our clarity.

References

Bourdieu, Pierre. 1986. "The Forms of Capital." In *Handbook of Theory and Research for the Sociology of Education*, edited by J. G. Richardson, 241–258. New York: Greenwood.

Brown, Wendy. 2015. *Undoing the Demos: Neoliberalism's Stealth Revolution*. New York: Zone Books.

Koob, George F., and Michel Le Moal. 2001. "Drug Addiction, Dysregulation of Reward, and Allostasis." *Neuropsychopharmacology* 24(2):97–129.

Polanyi, Karl. 1944. *The Great Transformation*. Boston: Beacon Press.

Wilkinson, Richard, and Kate Pickett. 2009. *The Spirit Level: Why Greater Equality Makes Societies Stronger*. New York: Bloomsbury Press.

Chapter 11

The Trauma of the 90%

Throughout the twentieth century, a quiet shift occurred in the structure of opportunity. For a brief historical window, many individuals in the United States—particularly those born between 1946 and 1964, often referred to as the Baby Boomer generation—entered adulthood during one of the most economically favorable periods in modern history.

College tuition was relatively affordable. Wages rose alongside productivity. Housing prices were low relative to income. Public investment in infrastructure, education, and social mobility remained strong. For many households, it was possible to build stability through a single income. A modest job could support a family, purchase a home, and allow for savings.

This period created a powerful narrative: that success was primarily the result of individual effort. If one worked hard enough, prosperity would follow.

But what is often forgotten is that these outcomes were not merely the product of individual virtue. They were the result of **specific historical conditions**—conditions that no longer exist for the generations that followed.

By the time Millennials and Gen Z entered adulthood, the structural landscape had changed dramatically.

Housing costs skyrocketed relative to wages. Higher education became increasingly expensive, often requiring decades of debt repayment. Secure employment gave way to temporary contracts, gig work, and precarious labor markets. Healthcare costs expanded while public safety nets shrank. Meanwhile, wealth concentrated at unprecedented levels.

Younger generations did not simply encounter a more difficult version of the same system. They encountered a **different system altogether**.

This divergence between generational realities has created a quiet but pervasive psychological wound: the feeling that one is being judged according to rules that no longer apply.

When people who benefited from an earlier economic structure insist that the same pathways to stability remain equally accessible today, the result is not simply a disagreement—it becomes a form of institutional misunderstanding that can feel intensely personal. Younger people often internalize the message that their struggle is evidence of individual failure rather than evidence of structural transformation.

This misrecognition helps explain why younger generations report such high levels of distress. Many are asked to do more than their grandparents—work longer hours, acquire more credentials, navigate higher costs for housing, healthcare, and education—and yet still fall short of meeting basic human needs with dignity. Too often, that distress is then medicalized or dismissed by professionals who ignore the social reality producing it, treating trauma responses to a traumatic world as private pathology.

The result is a shaming loop: structural deprivation is reframed as personal inadequacy, and the shame becomes an additional injury layered on top of the original harm created by greed.

This is where generational tension emerges.

It is not simply about age differences. It is about **historical context**.

Baby Boomers grew up in an era of expanding opportunity. Younger generations are coming of age during an era defined by scarcity narratives, competition, and economic precarity.

When these two realities collide, frustration grows on both sides.

Older generations may believe younger people lack resilience or discipline. Younger generations may feel that older leaders are unwilling to recognize how profoundly the system has changed for the worse. The very system the baby boomers founded.

Underneath these conflicts lies a deeper issue: **the concentration of economic and political power**.

Baby Boomers currently occupy a disproportionate number of leadership roles across politics, corporate governance, and institutional authority. Because demographic shifts occur slowly, this generation has held influence for decades. Many key decisions about economic policy, housing markets, education costs, and labor conditions have been shaped during this period.

This has produced a generational bottleneck in power.

Younger generations are often told to be patient—to wait their turn.

But waiting becomes increasingly difficult when the structures shaping one's life appear immovable and limiting.

For many people under forty, the future can feel suspended. Careers stall. Housing remains inaccessible. Families are postponed or abandoned entirely due to financial uncertainty.

The psychological consequences of this prolonged instability are profound.

A society cannot maintain collective trust when a majority of its members feel permanently excluded from stability.

This is the **trauma of the majority** and it will leave its mark on society as there will be a huge population drop since new generations can't afford to have children.

What happens when this generational transition eventually occurs?

Demographically, the Baby Boomer generation will gradually leave the workforce and positions of leadership over the next two decades. This shift will inevitably transfer wealth, property, and institutional power to younger generations.

But the direction of that transition is not predetermined.

Two futures are possible.

In the first scenario, the dominant narrative remains unchanged. Economic inequality continues to widen. Housing remains speculative. Education remains commodified. Healthcare remains inaccessible for many. Work becomes increasingly precarious as automation and global competition intensify.

If the underlying assumptions of the current system remain intact, the generational transition may change the faces of leadership without changing the structure of power itself.

The trauma doesn't simply end—it continues, accumulates, and compounds. In *What Happened to Humanity?* I argue that this kind of structural cruelty is not accidental. I wrote about the Club of Rome's long-term depopulation agenda, aimed at reducing Earth's population to 10% of what it is in elite policy discourse.

Whether one frames this as deliberate planning or as the predictable outcome of greed-built institutions, the ethical reality remains the same: systems that ration care, weaponize bureaucracy, and normalize abandonment produce preventable suffering at scale.

Younger leaders raised within the same scarcity-driven framework may reproduce the same competitive systems they inherited.

The second scenario is more hopeful, but it requires a shift in imagination.

Rather than interpreting generational change as a simple transfer of power, society could reinterpret it as an opportunity to renegotiate the social contract.

What would it mean to design systems around **human well-being rather than pure economic growth**?

What would education look like if its primary goal were intellectual development rather than debt-financed credentialing?

What would housing policy look like if shelter were treated as infrastructure rather than investment?

What would work look like if stability were considered a public good rather than an individual gamble?

What would work look like if we reduced bureaucratic paper trails and focused instead on presence and care?

These questions represent more than policy debates. They represent a cultural transformation in how society defines success, value, and security.

Younger generations have already begun exploring alternative narratives: cooperative economic models, community-based support networks, new approaches to mental health, and movements focused on sustainability and collective care.

These emerging frameworks challenge the assumption that relentless competition is the only path to prosperity.

They suggest that a different story may still be possible.

History shows that economic systems are not permanent. They evolve as societies renegotiate the balance between individual ambition and collective responsibility.

The coming decades may therefore represent not merely the passing of one generation, but a turning point in how opportunity itself is imagined.

The trauma of the 90 percent—the majority struggling within increasingly unequal systems—does not have to define the future.

But healing that trauma requires confronting a difficult truth: the narratives that once guided society may no longer be sufficient for the world that now exists.

The question facing the next generation of leaders is not whether change will occur.

It is **what kind of change we are willing to imagine**.

PART IV

BREAKING THE ADDICTION

CHAPTER 12

How Can We Recover?

A system cannot recover while it is still calling the disease "success."

That is the first Truth-Teller sentence we all need to explore. Recovery begins the moment we stop confusing domination with leadership, scarcity with reality, and accumulation with safety. A greed-addicted system survives by keeping people overstimulated, afraid, divided, and ashamed—too busy competing to notice that the rules are invented and the suffering is unnecessary.

So the first intervention is not policy. It is perception.

We have to name greed for what it is: an addiction—often a socially rewarded one. And when people are caught inside any addiction, the response cannot be admiration or moral shaming. It requires intervention, care, and boundaries: support that recognizes the underlying fear and disconnection driving the compulsion, while refusing to let the compulsion keep harming others.

On an individual level, people struggling with greed addiction can benefit from many of the same modalities used in addiction recovery—trauma-informed therapy, accountability structures, community support, somatic regulation, honest feedback, and practices that rebuild meaning beyond achievement. But lasting change cannot occur if the surrounding culture continues to validate the illness. An addicted person cannot recover while living inside an environment that constantly triggers the compulsion and calls escalation "excellence."

That is the deeper problem: the culture itself has been trained to invert reality—praising what is destructive, aestheticizing deprivation, calling numbness "professionalism," calling domination "leadership," and calling extraction "success." When a society treats addiction as virtue, recovery becomes an act of resistance. So the work is dual: support the individual, and dismantle the cultural narrative that keeps the addiction socially protected. Only when we stop celebrating the compulsions—only when we stop calling ugly good—can "enough" become thinkable, and healing become sustainable.

---

1) Truth-Teller Recovery Starts with the Nervous System

Greed addiction is not only economic. It is a nervous-system culture: high alert, comparison, urgency, constant proving. You cannot think your way out of a system that trains your body to panic. If your baseline state is threat, you will keep reaching for control. And in this society, control is sold as: money, status, property, productivity, dominance.

Recovery requires rebuilding an internal baseline where you can feel safe without the mask.

That is not soft. That is revolutionary.

When enough people can regulate without buying control, the system loses leverage.

Healing circles, shared practices of co-regulation, and spaces for constructive feedback are some of the ways we can hold more room for truth. That also means reclaiming the freedom to voice pain and frustration publicly—without having our concerns dismissed through "professionalism" or tone policing. When people are allowed to name what is happening, be witnessed, and metabolize anger and grief without being punished for having emotions, truth stops being an individual burden and becomes a collective practice.

---

2) Fasting from the System's Inputs

A recovery program always includes fasting—not necessarily from food, but from the triggers that keep the addiction alive.

Truth-Teller fasting can look like:

- fasting from constant news cycles that hijack attention
- fasting from comparison (especially algorithmic comparison)
- fasting from hustle language (the inner whip)
- fasting from self-optimization as a moral duty
- fasting from the daily stories—spoken and unspoken—that tell you you're behind, late, less-than, or unworthy

This is a detox from manipulation. And it is harder than it sounds. We need to reclaim rest as prayer. We need to practice gratitude for "enoughness".

Capitalism productivity and grind culture programming runs deep. So the practice has to be concrete: pause, name the gaslight, identify the blame shift, and retell the story from a truthful framework until the body can feel safe again.

---

3) Dancing Instead of Speaking: Returning to the Body's Language

Words are powerful, but in a greed-addicted society, language is also a cage. The system uses words—policies, metrics, categories, "professionalism," "productivity," "deserving"—to define who counts and who doesn't.

So part of recovery is remembering that human truth predates language.

There are forms of knowing that do not require debate:

- movement
- rhythm
- breath
- silence
- eye contact

- shared presence
- grief held in a circle without explanation

Dancing instead of speaking is not escapism. It is de-programming. It returns people to a shared nervous-system reality where care becomes visible and performance drops away. It becomes a way of expression. Perhaps, this is one reason so many of our tribal ancestors organized life around ceremony—music, singing, drumming, and dance were not entertainment at the edge of life; they were technologies of cohesion, regulation, and meaning.

When I imagine the future, I imagine every street becoming its own tribe. At night, after a day of work that is both productive and genuinely human—work that creates real bonds rather than mere transactions—people gather to eat, to move, to dance, and to restore one another. Each small community develops its own traditions, and no tradition is treated as superior to another. Being human means we create meaning, but that meaning is only alive in the context of our lived relationships, not as a permanent hierarchy. The goal is presence—like children, like animals—where the body is not an obstacle to truth but one of its clearest sources.

When we return to embodied communication, we interrupt the system's favorite trick: turning everything into an argument instead of a felt truth. Animals and babies remind us that language is not only words. They communicate through tone, proximity, rhythm, gaze, breath, and repair. We need to relearn that literacy. And I also believe we need to return to the realities that modern life hides from us: caring for children, caring for animals, and sharing the processes of birth and death. These experiences reconnect us to something older than the marketplace—the memory that life is cyclical, that death is not simply an ending but a passage, and that our lives are threaded together in ways we can only understand when we slow down enough.

---

4) Silence as a Technology of Truth

Silence is not emptiness. Silence is where the truth becomes audible.

A greed-addicted world keeps people constantly stimulated so they never have to hear the body's truth: *I'm tired. I'm scared. I miss people. I want tenderness. I want freedom. I want enoughness. I want to stop performing.*

The body speaks in sensations and tension, not speeches. You get sick, mentally and if you ignore it long enough physically. You only learn body's language when you slow down long enough to notice:

- constriction when something is false
- ease when something is aligned
- collapse when something is coercive
- aliveness when something is real

In Truth-Teller recovery, silence becomes a daily practice—not to "self-improve," but to remember **what we already know.**

Not the kind of knowing that requires a spreadsheet, a credential, or a paper trail to count as real—another kind. There are truths we carry somatically and instantly, without translation. I don't need to write an equation on paper to understand it while I'm holding complex physical relationships in my mind. The math is already embodied.

Think about driving or playing tennis. In real time, the body is integrating speed, distance, posture, force, timing, gravity, balance, and biology—continuous calculation that makes life possible every second. To reduce "legitimate knowledge" only to what can be formally explained on paper is not simply limiting; it is a kind of epistemic violence. It trains people to distrust what they know through lived intelligence.

When I first began composing classical music, I used to imagine Mozart and Beethoven as if they had notation software installed in their brains. But the deeper truth is simpler and more radical: we already come with certain "software," and with practice we can refine it. Silence is part of that practice. It is where the mind quiets enough for embodied knowing to surface—where we can hear the body's truth without immediately forcing it into institutional language.

---

5) "Unbelieving Money" Without Falling into Harm

Here's a Truth-Teller nuance: *unbelieving money* does not mean pretending bills don't exist. It means withdrawing moral authority from money.

Money is not truth.
Money is not worth.
Money is not love.
Money is not safety.

Money is a human-made measuring tool that has been promoted into a god.

Recovery starts when we stop letting money tell us who we are.

And now—about rent and not paying: I can't advise illegal actions like simply withholding rent without protections. But I still find it baffling that humans are the only animals that "pay rent" to exist on the earth. When an animal loses its habitat—through drought, fire, or flood—it searches for another place to settle. We, on the other hand, have built a world where people can lose shelter and still be prohibited from building new shelters. Then we perform sorrow on the news about "the homelessness crisis," as if homelessness were a natural law rather than a manufactured outcome. Homelessness is not inevitable. It is designed—through property regimes that treat shelter as an asset class, through laws that criminalize survival, and through systems that block people from meeting basic needs outside the marketplace.

Housing should not be a permanent extraction pipeline.

And there are lawful, collective ways people pursue that truth:

- tenant unions and collective bargaining

- lawful rent strikes with legal guidance and escrow plans (when conditions justify it)

- community land trusts, housing co-ops, mutual aid networks
- policy fights for rent stabilization, vacancy taxes, and social housing

The spirit is: stop consenting to extraction as normal.
The method matters just as much: protect people from avoidable harm while organizing for structural change.

---

6) Don't Cram Life into One Box

A greed-addicted system wants people isolated, boxed into private survival units: one household, one job, one screen, one identity that can be marketed.

We were never meant to choose one profession and cling to it for an entire lifetime. Work—like most human experiences—is supposed to evolve as we evolve. Jobs can shift to meet our changing needs, and we can begin a new hobby at any point and, if we choose, grow it into a livelihood. Work, education, and even location are not fixed identities; they are contextual tools that should serve a life, not imprison it.

Truth-Teller recovery widens life:

- more shared meals
- more communal childcare and elder support

- more collective creativity
- more "village-scale" interdependence
- more public grief and public joy

Because isolation makes people governable.

Connection makes people free.

---

7) Learn Life from Animals Again

Animals do not romanticize hoarding. They do not build empires that require other animals to starve. They live inside limits. They rest without guilt. They play without proving.

Truth-Teller recovery asks a radical question:
What if our "civilization" is less evolved than the nervous system of a mammal who knows how to stop when full, sleep when tired, and run when afraid without building a bureaucracy around fear?

Learning from animals looks like:

- returning to seasons and rhythms
- moving the body daily without monetizing it
- listening for instinctive "yes" and "no"
- resting as a biological right, not a reward

---

8) Play Like a Child

A greed-addicted system hates play because play is value that cannot be extracted.

Play is the nervous system practicing safety.

Play is meaning without profit.

Play is creativity without justification.

When adults return to play—drawing, singing, building, wandering, making nonsense—they reclaim a part of themselves the system depends on erasing: the part that knows life is more than earning. The part that knows what we can imagine we can bring to life, and thus we need to imagine a kinder world and take actions in alignment with that best version of the world image we can create in our minds.

---

9) Imagination as Prayer—and Why "The Law of Attraction" Must Become Collective

Imagination shapes behavior, attention, and what people believe is possible. A society that cannot imagine alternatives will accept brutality as realism.

This is where a Truth-Teller version of "The Law of Attraction" can be redeemed:

Visualization is not magic. It is orientation.
It trains the nervous system toward possibility instead of doom.

But the fatal flaw of hyper-individual manifestation culture is that it can become greed in spiritual clothing: *my abundance, my success, my specialness.*

Truth-Teller imagination has one condition:

It only counts if everyone is included.

Because we are interconnected. We share joy and pain whether we admit it or not. No private prosperity built on someone else's deprivation is stable—it is just delayed collapse.

So the prayer becomes:

- enough housing for all
- enough food for all
- enough safety for all
- enough dignity for all
- enough time to be human for all

And then we build structures that match the prayer.

---

10) What Recovery Looks Like at Scale

A system recovers when it stops rewarding the addiction.

That means:

- redefining success as sufficiency + care, not accumulation
- building economic floors (housing, healthcare, food, education) so survival isn't coercion
- protecting time (rest, family, community) from extraction
- teaching emotional literacy and nervous-system regulation as basic education, allowing curiosity
- making truth-telling safer than silence

And culturally:

- praising repair over domination
- praising tenderness over performance
- praising integrity over winning

---

11) The End Goal

The end goal of Truth-Teller recovery is simple and extremely difficult:

To become safe enough—inside yourself and with others—that you no longer need the mask.

Not because the world became perfect.

But because you built a life where your body can tell the truth without punishment.

When enough people reach that state, greed addiction loses its fuel.

Because it was never fed by money alone.

It was fed by fear.

And fear cannot govern people who have remembered they are already whole.

Chapter 13

Replacing "More" With "Enough"

The greed-addicted system trains people to chase "more" as if it were safety. More money, more status, more credentials, more control. But **enough** is a different category. "Enough" is not a number; it is a condition—when basic needs are secured, when the nervous system can downshift, when relationship is possible without performance.

Replacing "more" with "enough" is therefore not only moral or philosophical. It is **material**. If we want human beings to stop living as if they are one emergency away from collapse, we have to build ways of living that reduce coercion. That means access to food, shelter, and community without constant extraction.

This chapter offers a grounded route: **independent living without isolation**—a life that reconnects people to land, skill, and mutual aid while still staying connected to the world online.

---

1) The material foundation of "enough"

A system organized around scarcity forces people into dependence: on landlords, employers, insurance networks, and credential gatekeepers. In such a system, "choices" become narrow and expensive. This is why "enough" requires shifting the base layer: **food, shelter, and energy**.

A practical definition of "enough" looks like this:

- you can eat without panic
- you can sleep without fearing displacement
- you can access care without proving extremity
- you have at least one place where you don't have to perform

Without these foundations, "more" keeps masquerading as survival. And people keep competing, even when it destroys them.

---

2) Independent living: not the fantasy, the design

"Living independently" doesn't have to mean "living alone." In fact, isolating individuals is one of the ways the current system stays powerful. Independence can mean **material resilience** paired with **relational interdependence**.

There are several models that make this real.

A. Small-scale farming and homesteading (the "enough" economy)

Not everyone needs to become a full-time farmer. But many people can move toward **partial self-provisioning**—food systems that reduce dependence on high-cost markets.

A realistic entry path often looks like:

- start with one skill: soil, compost, irrigation, or animal care
- grow 10–30% of your food at first (not 100%)
- learn a "whole farm" plan: labor, costs, water, tools, market options
- scale only if your nervous system can stay regulated

B. Keeping animals (food + companionship + rhythm)

Animals are not just "production." They teach rhythm and limit—two things greed addiction destroys.

Common starter animals (when local laws allow):

- **chickens**: eggs, compost contribution, easy entry
- **ducks**: eggs + pest control in wet climates
- **goats**: milk, brush clearing, strong personalities (higher learning curve)
- **bees**: pollination + honey (requires skill and respect)

The deeper point: animals pull people out of abstract metrics and back into embodied reality: weather, hunger, rest, care, seasons. That shift alone can weaken the "more" spell.

C. Land models that resist speculation

If "enough" is going to be stable, it can't be at the mercy of land speculation. This is why **community land trusts** matter: they remove land from the speculative market and hold it for community-serving purposes with long-term stewardship structures (CLT Network 2025; Grounded Solutions Network 2025). Put simply: land is treated as a commons-like resource, not a casino chip.

This model pairs well with:

- tiny home villages
- cooperative farms
- community gardens
- shared workshops
- mixed-use community hubs

It's one of the clearest structural ways to make "enough" durable.

---

3) Staying connected online while living close to land

One fear people have about land-based living is isolation. But technology can be used in a different way than addiction and comparison.

If the goal is "independent but connected," the infrastructure matters:

- satellite internet for remote areas
- cellular hotspots and mobile routers in areas with coverage
- community Wi-Fi infrastructure in cohousing/ecovillages
- shared workspaces / makerspaces within rural towns

This matters because it allows:

- remote work income while reducing cost of living
- online learning (farming, repair, animal care, building)
- global connection without constant urban extraction
- finding "your people" beyond geography

The key is intentionality: using the internet as a bridge, not as a cage.

---

4) Finding people you "Vibe with" and then physically connecting

This is where "enough" becomes more than survival—it becomes life.

The system teaches people to find matches through performance: status, résumé, aesthetics, consumption. But energy-matching is different: it's about nervous system fit. Pace. Depth. Honesty. Values. Capacity for repair.

A practical pathway looks like:

1. **Find your people online first** (shared values, shared ethics, shared longing)
2. **Move toward physical proximity** (visits, residencies, short-term stays)
3. **Build small-scale interdependence** (shared meals, shared tools, shared child care, shared projects)

There are existing ecosystems for this. The Foundation for Intentional Community maintains directories for ecovillages, cohousing, and other cooperative living models, which is one of the most direct ways to search for aligned communities (FIC 2026).

This is where many people discover a missing truth: **their "social anxiety" was often a mismatch problem, not a defect problem.** They were forcing connection in places where their nervous system could never settle.

Safety Without the Mask

A greed-addicted society trains people to pursue false safety. It teaches that accumulation will protect you, that status will stabilize you, that power will make you untouchable. But the promise never completes, because insecurity is profitable. "More" becomes the substitute for safety, and the substitute becomes endless.

This is why the opposite of greed is not sacrifice. It is **enough**—not as a slogan, but as a condition: basic needs secured, dignity protected, nervous systems able to downshift, and relationships possible without performance. And the opposite of domination is not powerlessness. It is shared human flourishing—where protection does not require hierarchy, and security does not require someone else's deprivation.

So the final measure of recovery is simple and difficult: **the ability to feel safe without the mask.** Not safe because the world became perfect, but safe because you rebuilt self-trust, reclaimed embodied knowing, and found or created relationships where authenticity is not punished. When enough people can live from that place—where worth is not purchased, where truth is speakable, where "enough" is real—the system loses its leverage. The addiction breaks not by renouncing desire, but by recovering forms of life no longer organized around fear.

References

Community Land Trust Network. 2025. "What Is a Community Land Trust?" Community Land Trust Network.

Farm Service Agency (FSA). 2025. "Beginning Farmers and Ranchers Loans." U.S. Department of Agriculture.

Foundation for Intentional Community (FIC). 2026. "Intentional Communities Directory." Foundation for Intentional Community.

Grounded Solutions Network. 2025. "Community Land Trusts." Grounded Solutions Network.

National Institute of Food and Agriculture (NIFA). 2025. "Beginning Farmer and Rancher Development Program (BFRDP)." U.S. Department of Agriculture.

Starlink. 2026. "Starlink Roam." Starlink.

U.S. Department of Agriculture (USDA). 2022. "How to Start a Farm: Beginning Farmers and Ranchers." U.S. Department of Agriculture.

www.ingramcontent.com/pod-product-compliance
Lightning Source LLC
LaVergne TN
LVHW010621100826
845148LV00014B/3060

* 9 7 9 8 9 8 8 2 4 6 8 7 9 *